C000083087

WATCHFUL
HOUR

A Scriptural Companion
to Eucharistic Adoration

by
Fr Florian Racine

All booklets are published thanks to the
generous support of the members of the
Catholic Truth Society

CATHOLIC TRUTH SOCIETY
PUBLISHERS TO THE HOLY SEE

All rights reserved. First published 2017 by The Incorporated Catholic Truth Society 40-46 Harleyford Road London SE11 5AY Tel: 020 7640 0042 Fax: 020 7640 0040 © 2017 The Incorporated Catholic Truth Society.

Original edition Could You Not Watch with Me One Hour? *© 2014, Ignatius Press. Reprinted with permission. All rights reserved.*

ISBN 978 1 78469 192 9

Contents

STAGE 1

Introduction to the Itinerary

In his last encyclical, Pope John Paul II wrote:

> The mystery of the Eucharist - sacrifice, presence, banquet - *does not allow for reduction or exploitation*; it must be experienced and lived in its integrity, both in its celebration and in the intimate converse with Jesus which takes place after receiving communion or in a prayerful moment of Eucharistic adoration apart from Mass. These are times when the Church is firmly built up and it becomes clear what she truly is: one, holy, catholic and apostolic; the people, temple and family of God; the body and bride of Christ, enlivened by the Holy Spirit; the universal sacrament of salvation and a hierarchically structured communion… The treasure of the Eucharist, which the Lord places before us, impels us towards the goal of full sharing with all our brothers and sisters to whom we are joined by our common baptism.[1]

Holy Sacrifice	*Holy Communion*	*Adoration of the Blessed Sacrament*

- What are the three dimensions of the Eucharistic mystery?

- What is the meaning of the two terms "mystery" and "treasure" that John Paul II uses for the Eucharist?

- "The Eucharist builds the Church and the Church makes the Eucharist." (*Ecclesia de Eucharistia*, n. 26) What are the names given to the Church?

- "The treasure of the Eucharist…impels us towards [its] full sharing." Just what is this?

Here, the term "mystery" designates an effective action and presence of God in the Church, for the life of the world and the sanctification of souls. The "mystery" exceeds the intellect without, however, contradicting it. Jesus is really present in the Eucharist. All the sacraments are acts of Christ through which he gives us his grace. But, in the Eucharist, he is there himself, permanent, living, and acting, hidden under the appearances of the sacred Host. The itinerary will present the divine life of Jesus in the Blessed Sacrament, what he does there and what he expects of us. The word "treasure" reminds us that the Eucharist is our greatest treasure. St Augustine, in speaking of God, wrote about the Eucharist: "All-powerful that he is, he could make nothing greater; all-wise that he is, he could find nothing more admirable; all-wealthy that he is, he could not make a more precious present." In other words,

God cannot give us a greater gift than that of the Eucharist. In his omnipotence, he cannot bear greater witness to his love. He has nothing greater to offer. St Peter Julian Eymard said: "Happy the soul that knows how to find Jesus in the Eucharist and, in the Eucharist, all things."[2] Through the Eucharist, we enter into the great movement of love: "From the heights of the Trinity, the incarnate Word descends to man in the Eucharist in order that, through Communion, man may ascend to his final end, the most-lovable Trinity."[3]

Eucharistic grace "impels us towards…the full sharing…" of this treasure. In the context of the encyclical, the concern is the communal celebration of the Eucharist between all Christians who have received the same baptism. To arrive at this goal, we must work toward the re-establishment of full ecclesial communion. But we can understand it more broadly: we cannot keep this treasure for ourselves: on the one hand, it has to be announced to all, and, on the other, it has to drive us to give ourselves to others as Christ handed himself over for us. *Evangelisation* and *charity*, these are the two dimensions of the Church's mission.

Through different stages founded on biblical texts, the itinerary will present what the Eucharist is, what is fulfilled in the Holy Mass, what Communion and adoration are, and why and how to adore, for "true worshipers will worship the Father in spirit and truth, for such the Father seeks to worship him" (*Jn* 4:23). Through illustrations, Magisterial texts, and quotations from the saints, the adorer

8

will discover how to enter into the following movement: in adoring the Son, to be driven towards the Father to receive the Holy Spirit and thus become a missionary, by announcing this treasure and by sharing the charity that flows from it. And all this in the Church, who gives us the Eucharist and who lives from the Eucharist. The itinerary will also stress the spiritual attitudes required for entering into adoration "in spirit and truth" as well as the practical means for remaining faithful to prayer, despite inevitable times of dryness and purification. The adorer will learn to draw from this "spring of water welling up to eternal life" (*Jn* 4:14), which comes from the Eucharistic Heart of Jesus.

Each stage can be made during or after the weekly hour of adoration, with the aid of the Bible. It is a self-taught course, a school of adoration offered to every believer. Those responsible for adoration in a parish will be able to have successive evaluations with the adorers of their staff in order to clarify certain points or respond to their potential questions. Here is the outline of the itinerary offered:

• *Introduction* (*one stage*: the three dimensions of the Eucharist).

The Son: The Lord Comes to Me, He Calls Me, I Respond to Him (*twenty-seven stages*):

• *God Comes to Meet Me* (*seven stages*: the burning bush; the tent of meeting; God alone shall you worship, "choose life"; God frees me from idols; Elijah meets God on Mount Horeb; the calling of Samuel; the Incarnation, and the birth of Jesus at Bethlehem).

• *I Respond, by Faith, to His Love* (*seven stages*: everlasting love and the parable of the hidden treasure; "Come to me", the Eucharist is the invention of love; the anointing at Bethany; Martha and Mary and the great commandment of love; the haemorrhaging woman and the act of faith; modes of Christ's presence and extensions of the Incarnation; the shock of the bodily presence of the Resurrected One).

• *The Signs of the Covenant* (*thirteen stages*: covenants in the Bible; the memorial; the Holy Sacrifice of the Mass; the Paschal Lamb; divine mercy; parable of the marriage feast [baptism and confession]; marriage in the Bible; the Eucharist makes the Church [incorporation into the Church]; the suffering servant and kenosis; "I am the living bread" – John 6 parts 1 and 2; Isaac's blessing and transubstantiation; the tree of life recovered).

GOD COMES TO MEET ME

STAGE 2

The Burning Bush: Moses Adores God and Receives a Mission

Now Moses was keeping the flock of his father-in-law, Jethro, the priest of Midian; and he led his flock to the west side of the wilderness, and came to Horeb, the mountain of God. And the angel of the Lord appeared to him in a flame of fire out of the midst of a bush; and he looked, and behold, the bush was burning, yet it was not consumed. And Moses said, "I will turn aside and see this great sight, why the bush is not burnt." When the Lord saw that he turned aside to see, God called to him out of the bush, "Moses, Moses!" And he said, "Here am I." Then he said, "Do not come near; put off your shoes from your feet, for the place on which you are standing is holy ground." And he said, "I am the God of your father, the God of Abraham, the God of Isaac, and the God of Jacob." And Moses hid his face, for he was afraid to look at God.

Then the Lord said, "I have seen the affliction of my people who are in Egypt, and have heard their cry because of their taskmasters; I know their sufferings, and I have come down to deliver them out of the hand of the Egyptians, and to bring them up out of that land to a good and broad land, a land flowing with milk and honey, to the place of the Canaanites, the Hittites, the Amorites, the Perizzites, the Hivites, and the Jebusites. And now, behold, the cry of the sons of Israel has come to me, and I have seen the oppression with which the Egyptians oppress them. Come, I will send you to Pharaoh that you may bring forth my people, the sons of Israel, out of Egypt." But Moses said to God, "Who am I that I should go to Pharaoh, and bring the sons of Israel out of Egypt?" He said, "But I will be with you; and this shall be the sign for you, that I have sent you: when you have brought forth the people out of Egypt, you shall serve God upon this mountain."

Then Moses said to God, "If I come to the sons of Israel and say to them, 'The God of your fathers has sent me to you,' and they ask me, 'What is his name?' What shall I say to them?" God said to Moses, "I am who…am." (*Ex* 3:1-14)

In the Bible, it is always God who comes to meet man. It is he who, in love, takes the initiative for the encounter. He expects only our response. Here, "the angel of the Lord" represents God himself who visits his people. He chooses the form of a burning bush. For some Church Fathers, the burning bush prefigures the wonderful mystery of the *Incarnation*, in which the divine nature unites itself to the human nature without destroying it ("with neither confusion, nor separation") in the person of the Son. Present in the Blessed Sacrament, Emmanuel, the God who visits his people, is truly the burning bush. This fire also evokes the infinite love of Christ, which purifies, transforms, and heals. God calls Moses by his name. He invites him to a personal encounter, a relation of love, a heart-to-heart.

How does Moses behave before God? For what reason? The position of the body is fundamental in prayer before the Blessed Sacrament. By taking up a position that is too comfortable for the body (sitting, even slouching on one's kneeler or chair), the heart loses some of its vigour and strength. The soul grows lukewarm and finds itself in a state of slumber, unable really to pray. It is by putting one's body at prayer that one puts one's heart at prayer. To adore the Lord with all one's heart, with all one's soul, and with all one's strength (cf. *Dt* 6:4) is to adore the Lord with one's entire person, thus also with one's body. In the following passage from Revelation, John sees how God is adored in heaven. "To cast one's crown before the throne" signifies the adoration of one who offers his person, with all he has and all he is, before the divine majesty:

> The twenty-four elders fall down before him who is seated on the throne and worship him who lives for ever and

ever; they cast their crowns before the throne, singing, "Worthy are you, our Lord and God, to receive glory and honour and power, for you created all things, and by your will they existed and were created." (*Rv* 4:10-11)

The Latin etymology of the word "adoration" is *ad os*, or "toward the mouth", which refers to the kiss and, by extension, to love. To adore is to give back one's life to the Lord; it is to embrace him, because he loves us as we are. In adoration, we dare to approach him with the reverence of our body, the light of our faith, and the love of our heart. Since love always tends to humble itself and since the Lord makes himself so small in the sacred Host, the adorer is invited to humble himself before the divine majesty. Some bow profoundly, as Moses must have done before the burning bush. One of the remedies for tepidness and spiritual dryness in prayer is the quality of the bodily position.

Some practical advice: begin adoration kneeling, if possible by prostrating upon the floor for a few moments. Remain in this kneeling position (perhaps using a prie-dieu). If the position becomes painful, sit down! Do not hesitate to get back on your knees from time to time to get your heart back to adoration if distractions distance you from prayer. End adoration in the position that you took at the beginning.

God gives his name to Moses. How is the name of God to be understood? This name is mysterious, unpronounceable.

We cannot name that which exceeds us, that which we cannot grasp or understand. In the Bible, one's name signifies one's mission. It characterises the person. Here the name "I am who am" recalls that God alone exists in himself and that God needs nothing and no one in order to exist. To the contrary, God, the source of being, of every being, keeps all that lives in existence. From the sacred Host, the Lord Jesus supports the universe. How can we not marvel before the Host, which contains in its entirety what the universe cannot contain! If the earth revolves around the sun, the cosmos revolves around the Host! To approach it in faith is to hold oneself in the heart of the world. The Host is our heaven on Earth. It is God who gives himself, our Alpha and our Omega, our beginning and our end. It is the resurrected Body of Christ, Saviour of the world.

From this encounter with God, Moses will receive a mission. What precisely is this mission? What is the mission that God gives us, following our encounter with Jesus, present in the sacred Host?

I warmly encourage the faithful to adore Christ, present in the Blessed Sacrament of the altar, letting him heal our consciences and purify us, enlighten us and unite us. In their encounter with him, Christians will find strength for their spiritual life and their mission in the world. In fact, in communing heart to heart with the divine Teacher, they will discover the Father's infinite love and will be true worshipers in spirit and in truth. Their faith in him will be revitalised; they will enter into God's mystery and be profoundly transformed by Christ. In their trials and in joys, they will conform their life to the mystery of our Saviour's cross and Resurrection… Every day they will become more and more sons and daughters in the Son. Then, love will be spread through them in human hearts, in order to build up the Body of Christ which is the Church to establish a society of justice, peace and brotherhood. They will be intercessors for all humanity, because every soul which is lifted up to God also lifts up the world and mysteriously contributes to the salvation freely offered by our Father in heaven.[4]

STAGE 3

The Tent of Meeting and the Pillar of Fire: Speaking with Jesus as a Friend

And the Lord went before them by day in a pillar of cloud to lead them along the way, and by night in a pillar of fire to give them light, that they might travel by day and by night; the pillar of cloud by day and the pillar of fire by night did not depart from before the people. `(*Ex* 13:21-22)

Now Moses used to take the tent and pitch it outside the camp, far off from the camp; and he called it the tent of meeting. And every one who sought the Lord would go out to the tent of meeting, which was outside the camp. Whenever Moses went out to the tent, all the people rose up, and every man stood at his tent door, and looked after Moses, until he had gone into the tent. When Moses entered the tent, the pillar of cloud would descend and stand at the door of the tent, and the Lord would speak with Moses. And when all the people saw the pillar of cloud standing at the door of the tent, all the people would rise up and worship, every man at his tent door. Thus the Lord used to speak to Moses face to face, as a man speaks to his friend. When Moses turned again into the camp, his servant Joshua the son of Nun, a young man, did not depart from the tent. (*Ex* 33: 7-11)

During the crossing of the desert, God protected and accompanied his people. In what manner did God accompany them? God did not address himself directly to the Israelites; rather, he spoke to them through Moses. Moses interceded for them. He met personally with God in the tent of meeting, presenting the requests of the people. What sort of relation was there between God and Moses within this tent of meeting?

We all know that the more we love someone, the more we want to be with this person. Parents' joy is to be with their children; grandparents' to be with their grandchildren; two young people who love each other want to marry in order to spend their life together. It is the same for the most beautiful mystery of our Catholic faith: the Real Presence of Jesus in the Blessed Sacrament. He remains with us day and night in the tabernacle, because he loves us so much that he never wants to leave us. He says: "I am with you always" (*Mt* 28:20), "for where your treasure is, there will your heart be also" (*Lk* 12:34). In other words, we are his treasure. Thus Jesus is here in person with his Heart burning with infinite love for us in the Blessed Sacrament.

The Curé of Ars often pointed to the tabernacle, saying: "Jesus is really there, and if you knew how much he loves you, you would be the happiest person in the world." More than anything on Earth, God wants us to be happy and to come near to him, because true happiness is knowing true love:

> a love that never changes…
> a love that has neither limits nor conditions…
> a love that is always there…
> this love awaits us in the Blessed Sacrament.

Pope St John Paul II says: "Jesus waits for us in this sacrament of love",[5] where he repeats his eternal call: "Could you not watch with me one hour?" (*Mt* 26:40)

And Jesus wishes all the world to know that an hour of adoration is easy to do, because Jesus is truly the easiest person in the world to meet and to love. You can help yourself with a prayer book, meditate on sacred writings, pray the Rosary – thus loving Jesus with the very Heart of Mary. You can also simply speak to Jesus as to a friend, in silence. It may happen that you are so tired that you do not wish to do anything but sit down and rest while feeling the sweet peace that comes from the simple fact of being in the presence of him whom you love most, Jesus in the Blessed Sacrament, who says: "Cast all your anxieties on [God], for he cares about you" (*1 P* 5:7); "My peace I give to you" (*Jn* 14:27).

St Thérèse of Lisieux wrote: "O darling, think, then, that Jesus is there in the tabernacle expressly for *you*, for *you alone*; He is burning with the desire to enter your heart"; [6]

"the nature of love is to humble oneself";[7] "In order that Love be fully satisfied, it is necessary that It lower Itself to nothingness and transform this nothingness into *fire*."[8]

Spiritual advice: "Consider your allotted hour of adoration as an hour of paradise; go there as one goes to heaven, to the divine banquet, and this hour will be desired, greeted with happiness. Sweetly keep alive the desire for it in your heart. Tell yourself: in four hours, in two hours, in one hour, I will go to our Lord's audience of grace and love; he invited me, he awaits me, he desires me."[9]

"No longer do I call you servants, for the servant does not know what his master is doing; but I have called you friends, for all that I have heard from my Father I have made known to you" (*Jn* 15:15).

Just as a lighthouse illuminates the night, guiding boats safely to port, so a chapel of perpetual adoration spreads the Light of Christ upon the parishioners, the city, and the whole world, guiding them on the path of sanctity and abundantly pouring forth the divine mercy upon all.

STAGE 4

"God Alone Shall You Worship"
"Choose Life"

Here is the beginning of the Ten Commandments:

"I am the Lord your God, who brought you out of the land of Egypt, out of the house of bondage.

"You shall have no other gods before me.

"You shall not make for yourself a graven image, or any likeness of anything that is in heaven above, or that is on the earth beneath, or that is in the water under the earth; you shall not bow down to them or serve them; for I the Lord your God am a jealous God...showing merciful love to thousands of those who love me and keep my commandments." (*Dt* 5:6-10)

"Hear, O Israel: The Lord our God is one Lord; and you shall love the Lord your God with all your heart, and with all your soul, and with all your might. And these words which I command you this day shall be upon your heart." (*Dt* 6:4-6)

"Behold, I set before you this day a blessing and a curse: the blessing, if you obey the commandments of the Lord your God, which I command you this day, and the curse, if you do not obey the commandments of the Lord your God, but turn aside from the way which I command you this day, to go after other gods which you have not known." (*Dt* 11:26-28)

The first, great commandment of God to the people of Israel is given in Deuteronomy 6:4. What is it? Hearing the Word of God is a question of life or death for Israel. The people, moreover, have experience of this in the desert. Without God, the desert remains a place of desolation and death. But through the hearing of the Word, the desert becomes the privileged place of encounter with the Lord. God offers his people ten words of life to help them pass from slavery to freedom. God does not give the Ten Commandments to hold sway over his people, which would amount to a new form of slavery and submission (cf. *Dt* 5). On the contrary, God gives ten words of life, to free his people from idols and teach them to love in truth.

In Deuteronomy 11:26-28, God confronts man with his own freedom and responsibility. God shows two paths: one brings happiness, and one leads to unhappiness. The path of happiness consists in faithfulness to God and to his words of life (the Commandments). He who chooses it receives the bounty of divine blessing. But man can misuse his freedom and follow the opposite path, a path without God. On this path, God cannot give his blessing. To reject the Lord is to cut oneself off from his blessings.

The Deuteronomist even speaks of a curse: apart from God, nothing good can come. How does Jesus recall this in John 15:5?

In the text of Paul VI below, what is the "living heart... of our churches"? How does the pope qualify adoration? What should our response to this presence be?

> The unique and indivisible existence of the Lord glorious in heaven is not multiplied, but is rendered present by the sacrament in the many places on earth where Mass is celebrated. And this existence remains present, after the sacrifice, in the Blessed Sacrament, which is, in the tabernacle, the living heart of each of our churches. And it is our very sweet duty to honour and adore in the blessed Host which our eyes see, the Incarnate Word whom they cannot see, and who, without leaving heaven, is made present before us.[10]

When speaking of Eucharistic adoration, it is common to remark that it prolongs what is celebrated at Mass. This is true. Nevertheless, let us not forget that in the Bible God invites his people to adoration long before having instituted the Holy Mass. To adore God alone, this is the first commandment. This goes back even to creation. Adoring God is a "very sweet duty".[11] A "duty" because every man must recognise in God his Creator and the source of his being. It is a duty of divine justice to adore our Creator, our Saviour, him in whom every man finds his existence. We cannot speak of social justice if it is not founded on divine justice, that is, on the adoration of the one God. Adoring is thus a duty, but Paul VI adds an adjective: "sweet". In what way is our adoration "sweet"?

Adoration is awestruck submission before the majesty of God. Thanks to revelation, the Christian knows that his adoration must pass through Jesus to return to God: "I am the way, and the truth, and the life; no one comes to the Father, but by me" (*Jn* 14:6). Jesus's whole life was a life of adoration of the Father. Jesus leaves his great adoration of the Father in the tabernacle. He wants to bring the whole Church there. In adoring the Eucharist, we enter into Jesus's adoration of his Father.

The book of Revelation centres on the adoration of God and of the Lamb. In its sacrificial presence, "the Lamb" signifies Jesus, who completely hands himself over to save us and who alone deserves the honour, glory, and praise of each man.

I saw another angel flying in mid-heaven, with an eternal gospel to proclaim to those who dwell on earth, to every nation and tribe and tongue and people; and he said with a loud voice, "Fear God and give him glory, for the hour of his judgement has come; and worship him who made heaven and earth, the sea and the fountains of water." (*Rv* 14:6-7)

In this passage, the angel is the messenger. That he is flying in heaven shows that his message is above all others. It is an "eternal gospel". He invites mankind to the adoration of God. Adoration is the first and most fundamental act of every man. In adoring, man discovers the Father, welcomes the Son, and lets himself be filled by the Spirit who gives life.

"Judgement" (cf. *Rv* 14:7) in the Bible should neither scare us nor give rise to a servile fear. God judges by revealing himself and in revealing to all his light and truth. God judges by showing himself as he is: a God who is all love. But also, a God jealous for the love of his children. For our salvation is too precious to the Father for him to endure seeing us turn away from him and attach ourselves to what is passing, what cannot fulfil. God wants all our heart. He wants to fill it with his charity in giving it the capacity to love our neighbour, even the least lovable.

Today in Rome, a monument is dedicated to Victor Emmanuel II. In tribute to his efforts for the unification of Italy, two soldiers make up an honour guard day and night before a large statue. Many other countries do the same to commemorate their hero. Should we not give as much honour to the "King of kings and Lord of lords" (*Rv* 19:16); not to a statue but to the living God, present in the Blessed Sacrament? For Scripture says: "Worthy is the Lamb who was slain, to receive…honour and glory and blessing" (*Rv* 5:12) "day and night within his temple" (*Rv* 7:15), for "by your blood you ransomed men for God" (*Rv* 5:9). And the book of Revelation reminds us that when we proclaim Jesus King by giving him the glory that belongs to his name, he takes possession of his kingdom.

It is God's love for man that created the world. It will be man's love for the Son of God in the Blessed Sacrament that will recreate the world and bring the advent of "a new heaven and a new earth" (*Rv* 21:1). For Jesus said to St Margaret Mary: "I thirst, and with a thirst so ardent to be loved by men in the Blessed Sacrament that this thirst consumes me, and I find no one who, in accordance with my desire, strives to quench it, by giving some return to my love",[12] but "I will reign by the all-powerfulness of my Heart, and you will see the magnificence of my love."[13]

STAGE 5

God Frees Me from Idols

In the Bible, the word "idol" means "breath". An idol is a passing breath of air. Ephemeral, an idol claims to fill the heart but shows itself to be powerless. It is only an illusion, a mirage. All that we love before God or more than God, these are our idols. In themselves, they may be worthy of esteem and love. But they cannot assume more importance than God. For all idols will pass, but God, his Word, his Love, will remain eternally:

> "Do not think that I have come to abolish the law and the prophets; I have come not to abolish them but to fulfil them. For truly, I say to you, till heaven and earth pass away, not an iota, not a dot, will pass from the law until all is accomplished." (*Mt* 5:17-18)

Going through the beginning of the book of Ecclesiastes (cf. chapters 1-3), name some of the vanities or idols listed by Qoheleth: "Vanity of vanities! All is vanity" (*Qo* 1:2).

Note how the author ends his meditation: "All has been heard. Fear God, and keep his commandments; for this is the whole duty of man" (*Qo* 12:13). Fear, in the Bible, is the attitude that pushes us to seek God and to receive his will. God loves us. He shows us what leads to happiness through his commandments, his words of love. To fear God is to respond to his invitation of love by following his ways. By listening to the Word of God and by putting it into practice, man discovers a path of unhoped-for freedom and happiness. In opposition to idols that pass away and only give the impression of happiness, God, his Word, his Love, will never pass away. St Augustine said: "You have made us for yourself, and our heart is restless until it rests in you."[14]

Let us return to the book of Exodus. When God had finished speaking with Moses on Mount Sinai, he gave him the two tables of the Covenant, tables of stone, written with the finger of God:

> When the people saw that Moses delayed to come down from the mountain, the people gathered themselves together to Aaron, and said to him, "Up, make us gods, who shall go before us; as for Moses, the man who brought us up out of the land of Egypt, we do not know what has become of him." And Aaron said to them, "Take off the rings of gold which are in the ears of your wives, your sons, and your daughters, and bring them to me." So all the people took off the rings of gold which were in their ears, and brought them to Aaron. And he received the gold at their hand, and fashioned it with a graving tool, and made a molten calf; and they said, "These are your gods, O Israel, who brought you up out

of the land of Egypt!" When Aaron saw this, he built an altar before it; and Aaron made proclamation and said, "Tomorrow shall be a feast to the Lord." And they rose up early the next day, and offered burnt offerings and brought peace offerings; and the people sat down to eat and drink, and rose up to play. And the Lord said to Moses, "Go down; for your people, whom you brought up out of the land of Egypt, have corrupted themselves; they have turned aside quickly out of the way which I commanded them; they have made for themselves a molten calf, and have worshiped it and sacrificed to it, and said, 'These are your gods, O Israel, who brought you up out of the land of Egypt!'" (*Ex* 32:1-8)

The people of Israel crossed the desert, passing from slavery to freedom. To what form of slavery were they submitted in Egypt? To what new form of slavery did they submit themselves by worshipping a golden calf? Worship of the one God frees man from every alienation that closes him in upon himself.

Let us not forget that the first request that God, from the burning bush, made to Pharaoh through the intermediary of Moses was: "Let us go a three days' journey into the wilderness, that we may sacrifice to the Lord our God" (*Ex* 3:18). Even before bringing up the physical liberation from the slavery imposed by the Egyptians, God wanted to free his people from a much more tragic slavery: that which consists in adoring false gods. Since Egypt worshipped certain animals (the ram, the calf, the bull), ranking them as divine, God asked his people to go out into the desert on a three day journey, far from the sight of the Egyptians, to sacrifice these animals. For the chosen people, this gesture meant a radical rejection of the worship of these animals. Since Pharaoh refused this request of Moses, God would bring his people out of the oppression of Egypt through the ten terrible plagues. For decades afterward, in the context of his divine education, God requested that his people sacrifice these animals, considered divinities by the surrounding peoples, so that there was never a risk that they be worshipped anew. Thus their heart was free for the adoration of the one God.

For a moment, let us ask the Spirit to show us the idols in our life. Afterwards, let us receive Benedict XVI's invitation to adore the Eucharist so as to be delivered from these idols and enter into the true freedom of the children of God:

> We cannot forget the beginning of the "Decalogue", the Ten Commandments, where it is written: "I am the Lord your God, who brought you out of the land of Egypt, out of the house of bondage. You shall have no other gods before me" (*Ex* 20:2-3). Here we find the meaning of the third constitutive element of *Corpus Christi*: kneeling in adoration before the Lord. Adoring the God of Jesus Christ, who out of love made himself bread broken,

is the most effective and radical remedy against the idolatry of the past and of the present. Kneeling before the Eucharist is a profession of freedom: those who bow to Jesus cannot and must not prostrate themselves before any earthly authority, however powerful. We Christians kneel only before God or before the Most Blessed Sacrament because we know and believe that the one true God is present in it, the God who created the world and so loved it that he gave his Only Begotten Son (cf. *Jn* 3:16). We prostrate ourselves before a God who first bent over man like the Good Samaritan to assist him and restore his life, and who knelt before us to wash our dirty feet. Adoring the Body of Christ means believing that there, in that piece of Bread, Christ is really there, and gives true sense to life, to the immense universe as to the smallest creature, to the whole of human history as to the most brief existence. Adoration is prayer that prolongs the celebration and Eucharistic communion and in which the soul continues to be nourished: it is nourished with love, truth, peace; it is nourished with hope, because the One before whom we prostrate ourselves does not judge us, does not crush us but liberates and transforms us.[15]

In the following passage, God addresses himself to one of the churches founded by John. The "sharp two-edged sword" is the living Word of God. It wishes to free us from our idols, which make us slaves. Here God reproaches his people for having a divided heart and for receiving the foreign teachings of false gods. Every sin leads us astray from true love and enslaves us. The Word of God reveals to man his own identity and how to become free. In his eagerness for the salvation of every man, God comes to free us and make us his children.

"And to the angel of the Church in Pergamum write: 'The words of him who has the sharp two-edged sword. I know where you dwell, where Satan's throne is; you hold fast my name and you did not deny my faith even in the days of Antipas my witness, my faithful one, who was killed among you, where Satan dwells. But I have a few things against you: you have some there who hold the teaching of Balaam, who taught Balak to put a stumbling block before the sons of Israel, that they might eat food sacrificed to idols and practise immorality. So you also have some who hold the teaching of the Nicolaitans. Repent then. If not, I will come to you soon and war against them with the sword of my mouth. He who has an ear, let him hear what the Spirit says to the churches. To him who conquers I will give some of the hidden manna.'" (Rv 2:12-17)

STAGE 6

Elijah Meets God on Mount Horeb
Prayer – Adoration

[Elijah] walked...forty days and forty nights to Horeb the mount of God. And there he came to a cave, and lodged there; and behold, the word of the Lord came to him, and he said to him, "What are you doing here, Elijah?" He said, "I have been very jealous for the Lord, the God of hosts; for the sons of Israel have forsaken your covenant, thrown down your altars, and slain your prophets with the sword; and I, even I only, am left; and they seek my life, to take it away." And he said, "Go forth, and stand upon the mount before the Lord." And behold, the Lord passed by, and a great and strong wind tore the mountains, and broke in pieces the rocks before the Lord, but the Lord was not in the wind; and after the wind an earthquake, but the Lord was not in the earthquake; and after the earthquake a fire, but the Lord was not in the fire; and after the fire a still small voice. And when Elijah heard it, he wrapped his face in his mantle and went out and stood at the entrance of the cave. And behold, there came a voice to him, and said, "What are you doing here, Elijah?" He said, "I have been very jealous for the Lord, the God of hosts; for the sons of Israel have forsaken your covenant, thrown down your altars, and slain your prophets with the sword; and I, even I only, am left; and they seek my life, to take it away." And the Lord said to him, "Go, return on your way to the wilderness of Damascus; and when you arrive, you shall anoint Hazael to be king over Syria." (*1 K* 19: 8-15)

The prophet Elijah is the last remaining defender of the one God, of the God of Abraham, Isaac, and Jacob. He proclaims this God who brought his people out of Pharaoh's slavery, this God who spoke to Moses in the desert and who fed his people manna so that they might come to the Promised Land. Elijah becomes the guardian of the Covenant, of faithfulness to God, of adoration of the one God, and of the purity of the faith. Why does Elijah choose mount Horeb (cf. *Ex* 3; *Stage 2*)? God shows himself to Moses in a burning bush. How does he show himself to Elijah?

This unassuming encounter with God reconfirms Elijah in his vocation. Let us note well the contrast between the sweetness of the divine encounter and the radical nature of the prophet Elijah's mission! What is this mission? Let us beseech God to show us what he expects of us after the sweet encounter with Jesus in the Blessed Sacrament.

God acts, not by noise, thunder, strikes of lightning, exterior power, but in the silence of the heart. He seeks, not fusion, but intimacy. Adoration is a "face-to-face" that leads to a "heart-to-heart". Here are the definitions of Carmelite prayer and of Eucharistic adoration:

"Contemplative prayer…in my opinion is nothing else than a close sharing between friends; it means taking time frequently to be alone with him who we know loves us." (St Teresa of Avila).[16]

> The object of Eucharistic adoration is the Divine Person of our Lord Jesus Christ present in the Most Blessed Sacrament. He is living; he wants us to speak to him; he will speak to us. And this conversation, which develops between the soul and our Lord, is true Eucharistic meditation; this is adoration. (St Peter Julian Eymard)[17]

Prayer is the "heart-to-heart" with Jesus. Adoration is the "face-to-face" that leads to the "heart-to-heart". Is it an unnecessary detour or a surer path for arriving at the same goal? Here are some reflections to help us understand better these two intimately related forms of prayer that the Church has never placed in opposition:

> In St Teresa of Avila's definition of prayer, each word is carefully thought out: friendship, fidelity, solitude, love of God. The mystics of Mount Carmel teach us that prayer consists in letting the Holy Spirit overcome the spirit of the disciple in such a way that his soul becomes totally united to God. This work of the Spirit is possible only in the soul of him who surrenders and

totally exposes himself to the work of grace. Adoration is not opposed to this path. Prayer itself calls us to adore the God to whom we give ourselves over like wood to fire. The Eucharist is the sublime means that God gives to man so that man may unite himself to God. The Church today heartily encourages the practice of Eucharistic adoration. It would be a shame to neglect it. To want to encounter God within us in a heart-to-heart without passing through the face-to-face of adoration requires a purification of the inner self and a solid formation, an ability to fight the passions without gloves, without which prayer runs the risk of leading us back to ourselves in an unfortunate introspection and not to God present within us. In the face-to-face of adoration, the resurrected body of Jesus purifies us, transforms us, and divinises us. It is pointless to oppose prayer and adoration. Within the Church, they complete each other, even if, at the individual level, each man is led according to the manner and the paths pleasing to the Lord. Thus each member of the faithful responds to God according to the inspirations that the Spirit whispers in his heart.[18]

Jesus explains the importance of Eucharistic adoration to Father Courtois:

It is under the Eucharistic radiance that you enrich your soul with my presence, I was almost going to say with my perfume… If I desire to be exposed to your gazes in the sacrament of my Eucharist, it is not for my sake, but for yours. I know better than anyone just how much your faith, in order to concentrate its attention, needs to be drawn to a sign that expresses a divine reality. Your adoration often needs to support the eyes of your faith through the sight of the consecrated Host. This is a concession to human weakness, but it is perfectly in accord with the laws of psychology… Here, it is the law of incarnation that is in play: so long as you are on earth, you are not pure spirits or abstract intellects; your whole being, physical and moral, must work as one in expressing your love in order to intensify this love. For certain privileged souls, it is possible to pass beyond this at least for a time, but why refuse to the masses of men of goodwill what can help them to pray better, to unite themselves better, and to love better?[19]

Adoration is not prayer; it is first of all contemplation of the mystery of the Eucharistic presence of Christ. Christ present in the monstrance is of course just as present in the tabernacle, but if the Church has us adore Christ in this way, it is to help us to enter more profoundly into the Eucharistic mystery and to live more intensely from his Real Presence.[20]

Benedict XVI highlights the importance of silence for the meeting of "I" and "Thou":

In life today, often noisy and dispersive, it is more important than ever to recover the capacity for inner silence and recollection. Eucharistic adoration permits this not only centred on the "I" but more so in the company of that "you" full of love who is Jesus Christ, "the God who is near to us".[21]

Well, it is very simple! When we adore Jesus in the Host, we adore him at once substantially present in the Host and – just as really, but spiritually – present within us. Heaven is at once on the altar and in our heart. We are like one of those lovely sponges plunged into the ocean. We are in the water, but the water is also in us: "Abide in me, and I in you." We let ourselves be filled on every side by the love of our God, from outside and from within. What is our role? It too is simple. Let us remember the words of St John: "[Jesus] came to his own home, and his own people received him not." If the lovely sponge retracts, closes itself, it cannot absorb the water that is offered to it… Let us also ask the Holy Spirit to help us open ourselves to the love offered in us and in front of us. Let us receive it, let us allow ourselves to act, let us abandon ourselves with confidence, "entirely awakened, in faith, to the creative action of God in us". Let us receive this offered love as much as possible, so that the over-saturated sponge that we become may overflow upon others. Such is the fount of living water that the Lord promised to the Samaritan woman.[22]

Finally, the Anomoeans used to say: "We can pray very well at home; we have no need of going to the church." St John Chrysostom responded: "You are in great error; for while you may, it is true, pray in your dwelling, you will not, however, do it as well as in the church!"[23]

STAGE 7

The Calling of Samuel

"Behind the second curtain stood a tent called the Holy of Holies, having…the ark of the covenant covered on all sides with gold, which contained a golden urn holding the manna, and Aaron's rod that budded, and the tables of the covenant" (*Heb* 9:3-4).

"And you shall command the sons of Israel that they bring to you pure beaten olive oil for the light, that a lamp may be set up to burn continually. In the tent of meeting, outside the veil which is before the covenant, Aaron and his sons shall tend it from evening to morning before the Lord. It shall be a statute for ever to be observed throughout their generations by the sons of Israel." (*Ex* 27:20-21)

Now the boy Samuel was ministering to the Lord under Eli. And the word of the Lord was rare in those days; there was no frequent vision. At that time Eli, whose eyesight had begun to grow dim, so that he could not see, was lying down in his own place; the lamp of God had not yet gone out, and Samuel was lying down within the temple of the Lord, where the ark of God was. Then the Lord called, "Samuel! Samuel!" and he said, "Here I am!" and ran to Eli, and said, "Here I am, for you called me." But he said, "I did not call; lie down again." So he went and lay down. And the Lord called again, "Samuel!" And Samuel arose and went to Eli, and said, "Here I am, for you called me." But he said, "I did not call, my son; lie down again." Now Samuel did not yet know the Lord, and the word of the Lord had not yet been revealed to him. And the Lord called Samuel again the third time. And he arose and went to Eli, and said, "Here I am, for you called me." Then Eli perceived that the Lord was calling the boy. Therefore Eli said to Samuel, "Go, lie down; and if he calls you, you shall say, 'Speak, Lord, for your servant hears.'" So Samuel went and lay down in his place. And the Lord came and stood forth, calling as at other times, "Samuel! Samuel!" And Samuel said, "Speak, for your servant hears."… And Samuel grew, and the Lord was with him and let none of his words fall to the ground. (*1 S* 3:1-10, 19)

Samuel was sleeping in the temple, near the ark of God. What did this ark contain? What is the origin of the candle that burns continuously before the tabernacle? "The lamp of God had not yet gone out" (*1 S* 3:3). This light was the last one shining in the temple. It prefigures the light that remains lit day and night before the tabernacle in our churches. This light not only signifies that the loving presence of Christ abides continuously in his Church, like a magnet that attracts everything to itself: "I will not leave you desolate" (*Jn* 14:18); "I am with you always, to the close of the age" (*Mt* 28:20). But this light also recalls that Jesus is our true Light in the Blessed Sacrament. He drives away the shadows of our heart and of our world.

"The presence of Jesus in the tabernacle must be a kind of *magnetic pole* attracting an ever greater number of souls enamoured of him, ready to wait patiently to hear his voice and, as it were, to sense the beating of his heart."[24]

Jesus is the Bridegroom. The Church, represented by our parish community, is the Bride. The presence and thus continuous availability of Christ the Bridegroom to his Church-Bride calls for the total response of the Church-Bride to Christ the Bridegroom in the Eucharist. Through perpetual adoration, it is the whole community that returns love for love to Jesus, by showing up day and night before the Lord. Sadly, it is often the real absence of the community that responds to the Real Presence of Christ in the Eucharist.

Dina Bélanger, beatified by Pope St John Paul II in 1993, wrote in her journal:

If souls understood what treasure they possess in the divine Eucharist, it would be necessary to protect tabernacles with impregnable ramparts; because, in the delirium of a holy and devouring hunger, they would go themselves to feed on the Manna of the Seraphim.

Churches, at night as in daytime, would overflow with worshipers wasting away with love for the august prisoner.[25]

How does God call Samuel? And how does Samuel respond to him? God always calls by the first name. It is an invitation to live a personal, intimate relationship with our God, who alone can fill the heart. In this passage from Pope St John Paul II, how does God love us in the Eucharist?

The Eucharist is the sacrament of the presence of Christ, who gives himself to us because he loves us. He loves each one of us in a unique and personal way in our practical daily lives: in our families, among our friends, at study and work, in rest and relaxation. He loves us when he fills our days with freshness, and also when, in times of suffering, he allows trials to weigh upon us: even in the most severe trials, he lets us hear his voice.

Yes, dear friends, Christ loves us and he loves us for ever! He loves us even when we disappoint him, when we fail to meet his expectations for us. He never fails to embrace us in his mercy. How can we not be grateful to this God who has redeemed us, going so far as to accept the foolishness of the cross? To God who has come to be at our side and has stayed with us to the end? ...

Dear friends, when you go back home, set the Eucharist at the centre of your personal life and community life: love the Eucharist, adore the Eucharist and celebrate it, especially on Sundays, the Lord's Day. Live the Eucharist by testifying to God's love for every person.

I entrust to you, dear friends, this greatest of God's gifts to us who are pilgrims on the paths of time, but who bear in our hearts a thirst for eternity. May every community always have a priest to celebrate the Eucharist! I ask the Lord therefore to raise up from among you many holy vocations to the priesthood. Today as always the Church needs those who celebrate the Eucharistic Sacrifice with a pure heart. The world must not be deprived of the gentle and liberating presence of Christ living in the Eucharist!

You yourselves must be fervent witnesses to Christ's presence on the altar. Let the Eucharist mould your life and the life of the families you will form. Let it guide all life's choices. May the Eucharist, the true and living presence of the love of the Trinity, inspire in you ideals of solidarity, and may it lead you to live in communion with your brothers and sisters in every part of the world.[26]

Some practical advice: let us know how to respond like Samuel: "Speak, for your servant hears." Too often, we say to the Lord, "Hear, Lord, for your servant speaks"! Through adoration, Jesus wants to decentre us from ourselves to make us open to the divine will. When we enter into the chapel of adoration, let us know how to begin with love and not with our problems:

Begin all your periods of adoration with an act of love, and you will open your soul deliciously to his divine action. It is because you begin with yourselves that you give up on the way; or else, if you begin with some virtue other than love, you are on the wrong track. Does a child not kiss his mother before obeying her? Love is the only door to the heart.[27]

STAGE 8

The Incarnation and the Birth of Jesus at Bethlehem

Now the birth of Jesus Christ took place in this way. When his mother Mary had been betrothed to Joseph, before they came together she was found to be with child of the Holy Spirit; and her husband Joseph, being a just man and unwilling to put her to shame, resolved to send her away quietly. But as he considered this, behold, an angel of the Lord appeared to him in a dream, saying, "Joseph, son of David, do not fear to take Mary your wife, for that which is conceived in her is of the Holy Spirit; she will bear a son, and you shall call his name Jesus, for he will save his people from their sins." All this took place to fulfil what the Lord had spoken by the prophet: "Behold, a virgin shall conceive and bear a son, and his name shall be called Emmanuel" (which means, God with us). (*Mt* 1:18-23)

"And the Word became flesh and dwelt among us" (*Jn* 1:14).

Beginning with Adam, God saw that his greatness provoked resistance in man; that man felt limited in his very being and threatened in his freedom. This is why God chose a new way. He became a child. He made himself dependent and weak, in need of our love. Today, this God who has made himself a little child tells us, you can no longer be afraid of me, from now on you can only love me. In the table below, link the boxes of the different columns by connecting the bullet points.

If necessary, reread the passages of Matthew 2:1-12, Luke 2:1-20 and John 1:14 (see the table below). The verse "He dwelt among us" is literally translated as "He pitched his tent among us." This expresses the permanence of Christ's presence in the midst of his people. Thus Pope St John Paul II said: "The Lord Jesus has pitched his tent among us and, from this his Eucharistic dwelling, he repeats to each man and each woman, 'Come to me, all you who labour and are overburdened, and I shall give you rest' (*Mt* 11:28)."[28]

Jesus at Bethlehem		Today, Jesus in the Eucharist
	Mt 2:1-12	
Bethlehem ("House of bread")	• •	Tabernacle lamp
Manger	• •	My Saviour
Poverty of crib	• •	Adoration of Jesus in the Eucharist
The Magi render homage to the newborn	• •	My God
The star comes to rest over the place	• •	Food, living bread

Jesus at Bethlehem			Today, Jesus in the Eucharist
Gold	•	•	Church ("Body of Christ")
Frankincense	•	•	My King
Myrrh	•	•	Poverty of the altar
	Lk 2:1-20		
Crib, place where the newborn rests	•	•	Blessed are the poor in spirit (*Mt 5:3*)
Wrapped in swaddling cloths	•	•	Thanksgiving after Communion
Birth at Bethlehem	•	•	The joy of knowing oneself to be eternally loved
The shepherds receive Good News, a great joy for all the people	•	•	Announcing the love of Christ offered in the Eucharist
They made known that which had been told them	•	•	My Heart, Jesus's place of rest
Praise and glorifying God	•	•	Consecration at Mass
Mary kept all these things in her heart	•	•	Under the appearances of bread
	Jn 1:14		
He dwelt among us	•	•	Permanent presence in the Church (Tent)

Starting with the two etymologies of the word "adoration" given by Benedict XVI, find the principal fruit adoration bears in the soul:

> The Greek word is *proskynesis*. It refers to the gesture of submission, the recognition of God as our true measure, supplying the norm that we choose to follow. It means that freedom is not simply about enjoying life in total autonomy, but rather about living by the measure of truth and goodness, so that we ourselves can become true and good. This gesture is necessary even if initially our yearning for freedom makes us inclined to resist it. We can only fully accept it when we take the second step that the Last Supper proposes to us. The Latin word for adoration is *ad-oratio* – mouth to mouth contact, a kiss, an embrace, and hence, ultimately love. Submission becomes union, because he to whom we submit is Love. In this way submission acquires a meaning, because it does not impose anything on us from the outside, but liberates us deep within.[29]

The "mouth to mouth" of which the pope speaks expresses two different gestures: either the kiss between two lovers or the lifeguard's action upon a drowned person, breathing into his lungs so that he might regain his own breath. In adoration, Christ not only invites us into a real relationship of love with him; he also breathes into our heart his own breath, his Spirit, which gives vigour and strength to our interior life.

Archbishop Kébreau of Cap-Haïtien responds in an interview to the question, "What do you think of Eucharistic adoration?":

It is a time of encounter between the depths of our misery and the depths of God's love. It is there that I can know that I am loved by Christ who delivered himself for me. Everything is from him. He knows how to untie the knots that keep me in their grip. There, I learn how to be silent in the deepest part of myself in order to be transformed by the Holy Spirit, real problems resolving themselves at the foot of the tabernacle. Jesus said to Angela of Foligno: "Concern yourself with me, and I will concern myself with you." Adoration nourishes faith, trains it to avoid lapsing into unbelief or superstition. It is essential among this people that believes that it is being injured. Adoration is not a pharmacy but the gratuitousness of God's gift.

A meditation on Christmas, the Incarnation, and the Eucharist by Archbishop Fulton Sheen:

If we were naturally good and naturally progressive, there would have been no need of Christ coming to earth to make men good. Those who are well have no need of a physician. If all were right with the world, God would have stayed in his heaven. His Presence in the crib in Bethlehem is a witness not to our progress, but to our misery… Just as Christmas is a season for exchanging gifts with friends, so Our Lord came to this poor earth of ours to exchange gifts. He said to us, as only a good God could say: "You give me your humanity and I will give you my divinity; you give me your time and I will give you my eternity; you give me your weary body and I will give you redemption; you give me your broken heart and I will give you love; you give me your nothingness and I will give you my all."[30]

Humanism is impossible because it is too academic; "love of humanity" is impossible because there is no such thing as *humanity* – there are only men and women; the religion of progress is impossible because progress means nothing unless we know whither we are progressing. Philosophical systems, scientific constructions, and slogans leave the heart of man cold. Even a theory about love means little as long as it remains a theory. But let Love become personal in Some One, and then it pulls at every heartstring in the world. There is the secret of the appeal of the Incarnation. Love became incarnate and dwelt amongst us. Since that day hearts that have known what the Incarnation means can never content themselves with any system which asks us to adore the cosmos. Man never has loved, never will love, anything he cannot get his arms around – and the cosmos is too big and bulky. *That is why the Immense*

God became a babe in order that we might encircle him in our arms.[31]

This is why the boundless God continues to make himself small in the Eucharist. He wants to descend upon our heart and find the same love that he found at Bethlehem, from Mary, Joseph, shepherds, Magi. He comes in the sacred Host to become our centre! He wants us to love him with all our feelings, our affection, our will, and our intelligence, according to his words: "You shall love the Lord your God with all your heart, and with all your soul, and with all your strength, and with all your mind" (*Lk* 10:27). He will make us apostles of his Love!

I RESPOND, BY FAITH, TO HIS LOVE

STAGE 9

Everlasting Love and the Parable of the Hidden Treasure

"I have loved you with an everlasting love; therefore I have continued my faithfulness to you." (*Jr* 31:3)

"For God so loved the world that he gave his only-begotten Son, that whoever believes in him should not perish but have eternal life." (*Jn* 3:16)

"The kingdom of heaven is like treasure hidden in a field, which a man found and covered up; then in his joy he goes and sells all that he has and buys that field." (*Mt* 13:44)

"Again, the kingdom of heaven is like a merchant in search of fine pearls, who, on finding one pearl of great value, went and sold all that he had and bought it." (*Mt* 13:45-46)

How does the Lord love us? What is God's greatest gift for us? (see also *Ps* 36:8; *Ps* 63:4; *Rm* 8:35)

The parable of the hidden treasure can be read in two different ways, each enriching the other:

1. First, Jesus himself is our treasure. He is present in the Eucharist, our greatest treasure on earth. Here are the

words of Benedict XVI, spoken after having visited the "treasury" of a magnificent German cathedral:

Eucharistic adoration is an essential way of being with the Lord. Thanks to Bishop Schraml, Altötting now has a new "treasury". Where once the treasures of the past were kept, precious historical and religious items, there is now a place for the Church's true treasure: the permanent presence of the Lord in his Sacrament. In one of his parables the Lord speaks of a treasure hidden in the field; whoever finds it sells all he has in order to buy that field, because the hidden treasure is more valuable than anything else. The hidden treasure, the good greater than any other good, is the Kingdom of God – it is Jesus himself, the Kingdom in person. In the sacred Host, he is present, the true treasure, always waiting for us. Only by adoring this presence do we learn how to receive him properly – we learn the reality of communion, we learn the Eucharistic celebration from the inside. Here I would like to quote some fine words of St Edith Stein, Co-Patroness of Europe, who wrote in one of her letters: "The Lord is present in the tabernacle in his divinity and his humanity. He is not there for himself, but for us: for it is his joy to be with us. He knows that we, being as we are, need to have him personally near. As a result, anyone with normal thoughts and feelings will naturally be drawn to spend time with him, whenever

54

possible and as much as possible" (*Gesammelte Werke* VII, 136ff.). Let us love being with the Lord! There we can speak with him about everything. We can offer him our petitions, our concerns, our troubles. Our joys. Our gratitude, our disappointments, our needs and our aspirations. There we can also constantly ask him: "Lord send labourers into your harvest! Help me to be a good worker in your vineyard!"[32]

2. The parable can be read in the opposite sense: each person is Jesus's treasure. This other interpretation complements the preceding one. In this case, Jesus is the man who finds the treasure. How should we interpret "sells all that he has"? "buys that field"? Reread Revelation 5:9.

Note the "all". In his love for us, Jesus gave his body on the cross, in order to give us his body in the holy Eucharist and unite us to himself in his eternal glory. Just as wheat is crushed and ground to become bread, so Jesus accepted to be beaten, crucified, and pierced to become, for us, "the living bread which came down from heaven" (*Jn* 6:50). In delivering his body on the cross, Jesus said "I thirst." So too, in delivering himself entirely in the Eucharist, he says: "I thirst with such a terrible thirst to be loved by men in the Blessed Sacrament that this thirst consumes me."[33]

We can make the same double interpretation of these words of Jesus: "For where your treasure is, there will your heart be also" (*Lk* 12:34). On the one hand, the Eucharist is our treasure and must attract all the movements of our heart. On the other hand, we are his treasure. Jesus is thus here in person with his Heart burning with infinite love for us in the Blessed Sacrament. What do we make of this treasure?

The value of a single hour of prayer of adoration extends far beyond our capacity to think, to imagine, or even to desire. There is a story of a married couple who inherited a house, and, in the house, there was an old painting of a flowerpot. They were on the verge of throwing it out while they were tidying up to invite over some friends. Then, one of those invited, who worked in a museum, was drawn to the old painting on the wall that the couple had forgotten to throw out. He brought the painting to the museum to have it examined. It was not a copy but an original Vincent van Gogh, worth several millions; it made the couple one of the richest in Europe.

It is impossible to imagine the value of a simple hour of adoration. Too often Christ in the Eucharist remains in the tabernacle like that old painting whose value we have forgotten. And the monstrances are left in the dusty cupboards of sacristies. Yet Pope Leo XIII remarked about the Eucharist: "In this one mystery the entire supernatural order, with all its wealth and variety of wonders, is in a manner summed up and contained."[34] Like the young couple, we will be shocked, eternally shocked, upon discovering in heaven the value of an hour of adoration!

For it is measured by the degree of love that Jesus has for us in the Blessed Sacrament, which is infinite for him who says: "As the Father has loved me, so have I loved you" (*Jn* 15:9).

Let us end with a few comments from Blessed Charles de Foucauld: "Adoration of the Blessed Sacrament is repose, joy."[35] "Adoring the sacred Host: this ought to be the heart of every human being's life."[36] Charles, before the splendour of the Sahara, exclaims:

> Here we are at the gates of eternity. One almost believes that here, looking at these two infinities of the great sky and of the desert. You who like to see the setting of the sun, which, descending, sings eternal peace and serenity, you would like seeing the sky and the great horizons of this little Fraternity. But the best, the true infinity, the true peace is at the feet of the divine tabernacle. There, no more in an image but in reality, is all our good, our love, our life, our all, our peace, our beatitude: there is all our heart and all our soul, our time and our eternity, our All.[37]

> From his tabernacle, Jesus will shine upon these lands and attract adorers to himself... Does my presence do some good here? If it does not, the presence of the Blessed Sacrament certainly does much: Jesus cannot be in a place without shining.[38]

> I seek to do the will of Jesus from day to day and am in great interior peace. Do not worry yourself seeing me

alone, without a friend, without spiritual help: I do not suffer at all from this solitude, I find it very sweet: I have the Blessed Sacrament, the best of friends, to speak to day and night.[39]

Sacred Heart of Jesus, thank you for this first tabernacle in Tuareg country. Sacred Heart of Jesus, shine from the heart of this tabernacle upon this people who worship you without knowing you. Enlighten, lead, save these souls that you love.[40]

STAGE 10

"Come to Me"
The Eucharist Is the Invention of Love

"Come to me, all who labour and are heavy laden, and I will give you rest. Take my yoke upon you, and learn from me; for I am gentle and lowly in heart, and you will find rest for your souls." (*Mt* 11:28-29)

"Come away by yourselves to a lonely place, and rest a while." (*Mk* 6:31)

On the last day of the feast, the great day, Jesus stood up and proclaimed, "If any one thirst, let him come to me and drink. He who believes in me, as the Scripture has said, 'Out of his heart shall flow rivers of living water.'" Now this he said about the Spirit, which those who believed in him were to receive. (*Jn* 7:37-39)

"Follow me, and I will make you fishers of men." (*Mt* 4:19)

"Come and have breakfast." (*Jn* 21:12)

Jesus's prayer can be summed up in one noun: "Abba". His message begins with a verb: "Come". What does Jesus promise to those who approach him in the five invitations above?

Father Damien (1840-1889), apostle of the lepers, went to the island of Molokai to be near those he would call his brothers. There, he encouraged them to adore the Blessed Sacrament to find strength and hope in it despite the sufferings of their disease. Before he too caught and died from leprosy, he reminded his community of brothers that Jesus in the Blessed Sacrament was his best friend. From the tabernacle, Jesus says even today: "Cast all your anxieties on him, for he cares about you"; "My peace I give to you" (*1 P* 5:7; *Jn* 14:27). Here are a few of the saint's words:

> I find my consolation in the only companion of mine who never leaves me, that is, our divine Saviour in the holy Eucharist.
>
> It is at the foot of the altar that we find the strength we need in our isolation. Without the Blessed Sacrament, a situation like mine would not be sustainable. But with our Lord at my side, well then! I continue to be always happy and content. With this gaiety of heart and a smile on my lips, I work with zeal for the good of the poor unfortunate lepers, and little by little, without much fuss, good is done… [Jesus in the Blessed Sacrament] is the most tender of friends with souls that seek to please him. His goodness knows how to proportion itself to the littlest of his creatures as to the greatest. Do not fear, then, in solitary conversations, to speak to him of your woes, your fears, your troubles, those who are dear to

you, your plans, your hopes; do it confidently and with an open heart.[41]

The Eucharist, invention of love: at the end of his life on Earth, Jesus so loved us that he did not wish to desert us and leave us alone. However, he had to die on the cross to give us the gift of eternal life so that we might spend eternity with him in heaven in an indescribable joy. So Jesus made the greatest invention of all time, love's invention par excellence. The eve of his Passion, he took bread and said: "This is my body", then he took wine and said: "This is my blood." Take, eat, and drink. Jesus literally changed the bread and the wine into his own person. Why? To come dwell in our heart. This heart is so precious to him that he makes of it his new heaven on earth!

Immediately after having given his body to be eaten and his blood to be drunk, Jesus left for the Garden of Olives. He then asked his apostles to keep watch with him that they might not enter into temptation: Jesus came and found his disciples sleeping, "and he said to Peter, 'Simon, are you asleep? Could you not watch one hour? Watch and pray that you may not enter into temptation; the spirit indeed is willing, but the flesh is weak'" (*Mk* 14:37-38). In the Blessed Sacrament, Jesus remains with us to console us in our afflictions, accompany us in our solitudes, and make us victorious in our trials. He calls us to himself that he might give us the strength to persevere and the charity to love to the end. In other words, Jesus in the tabernacle is our travelling companion, our most faithful friend on earth.

Here are the words of Jesus to a woman religious, Josefa Menendez, who lived in Poitiers at the beginning of the twentieth century:

> The Eucharist is the invention of Love!… Yet how few souls correspond to that love which spends and consumes itself for them! I live in the midst of sinners that I may be their life, their physician, and the remedy of the diseases bred by corrupt nature. And in return they forsake, insult, and despise me… Poor pitiable sinners, do not turn away from me… Day and night, I am on the watch for you in the tabernacle. I will not reproach you…I will not cast your sins in your face… But I will wash them in my Blood and in my Wounds. No need to be afraid… Come to me… If you but knew how dearly I love you. And you, dear souls, why this coldness and indifference on your part?… Do I not know that family cares…household concerns…and the requirements of your position in life make continual calls upon you?… But cannot you spare a few minutes in which to come and prove your affection and your gratitude? Do not allow yourselves to be involved in useless and incessant cares, but spare a few moments to visit and receive this Prisoner of Love! [42]

Some spiritual advice: Let us love Jesus passionately, not only with our feelings, but also with our entire will. "So long as we do not have a passionate love for our Lord in the Most Blessed Sacrament, we will have done nothing."[43] "It is said: all that, it is just exaggeration. But love is nothing but exaggeration! To exaggerate is to go beyond the law. Well, love must go beyond the law."[44]

Here is the first part of St Anthony Mary Claret's meditation:[45]

Jesus speaks to me: My child, you do not need to know greatly in order to please me. It is enough to love me greatly. Tell me what you would say to your mother if she were here and she drew you upon her knees. Recount to me what you would recount to an intimate friend with whom you could never become bored. If, however, you desire some topics of conversation, here are some that you may find useful for each day of the week.

Have you no one to ask me to look after? Tell me the name of your parents, of your benefactors, of your friends. After each of these names, add what you would like me to do for them. Ask a lot, really a lot. I love generous hearts that forget themselves for others. Speak to me of all those who do you good, of the poor you would like to relieve, of the sick you have seen suffering, of the mean-spirited you would like to convert, of persons who have distanced themselves from you and whom you would like to bring back to your affection. For all of them, recite a fervent prayer; remind me that I promised graciously to hear every prayer that comes from the heart, and is it not a prayer from the heart that we make for those persons whom we love and who love us?

Have you no graces to ask me to grant you? If you wish, write a list of all your desires and come read it to me! Love of prayer would make you more fervent; humility would make you less touchy; patience would strengthen you against the fits of anger to which you let yourself give way; diligent work would prevent a host of angry mutterings; charity would make you more lovable... Have you no need of all these virtues? Tell me all these things, and entreat me to help you in the efforts you wish to make; I am the master of the goods of the soul; the goods of the body are also in my possession, ask me for them: health, intelligence, success. I can give everything, and I give it always, when these goods are useful for making souls more holy... What then do you wish, my child?

Have you no plans preoccupying you? Tell them to me in detail... Is it about your vocation? What do you think about? What would you like? Is it a question of pleasing your family? What do you want to do for them all? And for me, have you not a few ardent thoughts? Do you not wish to do some good to those around you? Tell me in whom you are interested, what is the motive driving you? What are the means you want to take? Reveal your lack of success to me; I will show you the reason for it. Whom do you wish to interest in your work? I am the master of hearts, my child, and I lead them sweetly wherever I wish. I shall place near you those whom you will need, be at peace...

Have you no troubles? Oh, my child, tell me your troubles with lots of details! Who has hurt you, who has injured your pride, who has hated you? Tell me everything; and then finish by adding that you forgive, that you forget, and I, I will bless you! Are you dreading something difficult? Is there in your soul that vague terror which is not rational but that torments you? Entrust yourself fully to my Providence. I am there; I am listening; I will not leave you... Are there hearts around you that seem less good to you, and whose indifference or forgetfulness distances them from you without your being aware of having done anything to hurt them? Implore me heartily for them...I will bring them back if they are useful for your sanctification.

(*Continuation of the meditation is in Stage 11.*)

STAGE 11

The Anointing at Bethany
The Great Service of Adoration

And while he was at Bethany in the house of Simon the leper, as he sat at table, a woman came with an alabaster jar of ointment of pure nard, very costly, and she broke the jar and poured it over his head. But there were some who said to themselves indignantly, "Why was the ointment thus wasted? For this ointment might have been sold for more than three hundred denarii, and given to the poor." And they reproached her. But Jesus said, "Let her alone; why do you trouble her? She has done a beautiful thing to me. For you always have the poor with you, and whenever you will, you can do good to them; but you will not always have me. She has done what she could; she has anointed my body beforehand for burying. And truly, I say to you, wherever the gospel is preached in the whole world, what she has done will be told in memory of her." (*Mk* 14:3-9)

Each hour of adoration is like a very pure ointment that we offer to Jesus. Why did the woman break a jar of very pure nard to pour over the head of Jesus? Note that the quality of the ointment expresses the quality of the love. Rather than keeping it for herself, she chooses to give it to Jesus. In the same vein, rather than keeping an hour of our week for ourselves, to attend to our own personal affairs, we can give it to Jesus by coming to adore him. And Judas becomes indignant: "What good can come of this waste?" – as the spirit of the world affirms today that spending time before the Blessed Sacrament is a waste or a loss of time. There are so many other ways to use our time. Yet Jesus responds: "Wherever the gospel is preached in the whole world, what she has done will be told." This act was so precious in the eyes of God and brought such glory to Jesus that the Holy Spirit wished this episode to be part of the Gospel! Likewise for us, for all eternity, God the Father will bless us for having loved his Son here on earth by spending an hour each week with him to give him love for love in the sacrament of his Love!

Adoration is a service. A service to the Divine Person of Jesus and a great service to mankind.

• Jesus remains in the Blessed Sacrament to give us the privilege of approaching him personally as so many people were able to do two thousand years ago in Galilee and Judea. By our adoration, we can love Jesus today, like the humble shepherds of Bethlehem, like the Magi who brought their gifts, or like Mary of Bethany who poured very pure nard over the head of the Christ. Adoring the Eucharist *is serving the Divine Person of Jesus today,* as the disciples did in their time. In this vein, St John Chrysostom said:

"How many say: I would like to see his face, his features, his beauty… But in the Eucharist, it is he himself whom you see, he himself whom you touch, he himself whom you eat. Think of that and adore, for it is the same who is in heaven and whom the angels adore!"[46]

• Also, in adoring, we *render a great service to mankind*: "Through adoration the Christian contributes mysteriously to the radical transformation of the world and the germination of the Gospel. Every person who prays to the Lord brings the whole world along with him, raising the world to God. Thus those who remain before the Lord fulfil a great service; they present to Christ all those who do not know him or who are far from him; in their name they keep vigil before him."[47] On the Cross, Jesus took our place. We take the place of him who has the greatest need of divine mercy by going to Jesus in a holy hour. Our adoration makes the Precious Blood of Jesus descend upon this person. The person obtains the graces necessary to return to God. In the Eucharist, Jesus says: "It is the will of my Father that no one be lost" (cf. *Jn* 6:39-40). Paul VI wrote: "The Eucharist is supremely effective for the transformation of the world into a world of justice, holiness, and peace."[48]

St John Paul II encouraged all to "meet him in adoration and in contemplation that is full of faith and ready to make reparation for the great faults and crimes of the world."[49]

Pascal Pingault, founder of the Bread of Life community, the "sixty-eighter" anarchist[50] who converted while prostrate before the sacred Host, was searching for a place to welcome the poor of our society. One day, during adoration, he was shattered by the passage of John's Gospel where Mary Magdalen anoints the feet of Christ with a precious ointment: "The poor you always have with you, but you do not always have me" (*Jn* 2:8).

> I understood that it was a prophecy for the persecuted Church, and our own, when his Eucharistic presence would be taken away from us… The Lord undoubtedly wants us to begin adoring him day and night, him first of all. The poor you will always have with you, but me, you will not have always. I understood the urgency to adore Jesus in the mystery of the Encounter. It was by experiencing his presence in the Eucharist that we would end up discovering him, adoring him also in our brothers – men, and above all the poor. It was by living from the Eucharist and in his Presence that we would come to meet those times of intense poverty that will be the end times – with the anguish and blasphemies of men, with their fears, their enormous sins, and their refusal of God. It was by contemplating day and

night his exposed Body – from which our eyes would be burned by light – that men who seek him would be deeply moved and would believe. Yes, it was time now to fulfil this mission that the Lord had assigned to us and to begin to prostrate ourselves day and night before him. I discovered at the same time that he was the poorest of all and that he desired us to take plenty of time beside him before letting us undertake whatever apostolate it would be and, above all, beside the poor.

From that instant, the community began perpetual adoration and obtained a house for welcoming the poor. God had put the priorities back in order: "You shall love the Lord your God with all your heart, and with all your soul, and with all your mind. This is the great and first commandment. And a second is like it, you shall love your neighbour as yourself" (*Mt* 22:37-39).[51]

In a call for adoration, Peter Kreeft writes:

Restoration of adoration of the Sacrament will heal our church, and thus our nation, and thus our world. It is one of Satan's most destructive lies that sitting alone in a dark church adoring Christ is irrelevant, impractical, a withdrawal from vital contemporary needs. Adoration touches everyone and everything in the world because it touches the Creator, who touches everything and everyone in the world from within, in fact, from their very centre. When we adore, we plunge into the centre of the hurricane, "the still point of the turning world"; we plug into infinite dynamism and power. Adoration is more powerful for construction than nuclear bombs for destruction.[52]

For if man with his created spirit can invent so powerful a weapon as the atomic bomb, how much more powerful will be the uncreated love of our resurrected Lord to bring eternal peace into the world!

Here is the second part of St Anthony Mary Claret's meditation (from *the end of Stage 10*).[53]

Jesus speaks to me: Have you no joys to tell me about? Why not let me in on your joys? Tell me everything that has happened since yesterday to console you, make you smile, bring you joy. Was there an unexpected visit, a reward that you did not think you merited, a fear that dissipated all at once, a success that you worried you were unable to obtain, a mark of friendship, a letter, a memento you received...

All of that, my child, it is I who have brought it about for you. Why would you not show yourself grateful for it...and would you not say again to me: Thank you! For gratefulness brings benefit, and the benefactor likes to be reminded of his generosities.

Have you no virtues to acquire, and have you no need of my help? Tell me your miseries, my child; confess yourself simply in my presence... Show me, by citing your frailties, how very sensual, prideful, touchy, self-centred, weak, lazy you are… Groan from how little you are familiar with renunciation, from how continually you abuse the graces that are accorded to you, from the pain that you give to your family, from the faults that perhaps you cause to be committed around you. My heart, my hands are full of treasures, and I want one thing only, to spread them with abundance. Ask me for my help… Each time you have acted lightly, without consulting me, without praying a little first, have you not acted less well, have you not perhaps done foolish things? You can do nothing, nothing without my protection, but with me, my child, you can do all things… Happy is the soul that feels me at its side, helping it, consoling it, protecting it!

Have you no promises to make me and orders to ask from me? I read to the depths of your heart, as you know. Men are fooled; God is not fooled. So be sincere… Are you resolved not to expose yourself again to this occasion of sin, to deprive yourself of things that bring you to evil, no longer to read this book? Do you want immediately to be good for the sake of this person who has hurt you? Do you want to act simply with everyone? Good, my child. And now go take up your work again. Be quiet, modest, charitable. I am waiting for you tomorrow; tomorrow, bring me a very pure and very devoted heart; tomorrow, I will have new favours for you.

STAGE 12

Martha and Mary
The Great Commandment of Love

[Jesus] entered a village; and a woman named Martha received him into her house. And she had a sister called Mary, who sat at the Lord's feet and listened to his teaching. But Martha was distracted with much serving; and she went to him and said, "Lord, do you not care that my sister has left me to serve alone? Tell her then to help me." But the Lord answered her, "Martha, Martha, you are anxious and troubled about many things; one thing is needful. Mary has chosen the good portion, which shall not be taken away from her." (*Lk* 10:38-42)

"You shall love the Lord your God with all your heart, and with all your soul, and with all your mind. This is the great and first commandment" (*Mt* 22:37-38) (Heart-to-heart with God).

"And a second is like it, you shall love your neighbour as yourself" (*Mt* 22:39) (Heart-to-heart with neighbour).

In this passage, Martha is presented as the mistress of the house. She wants to welcome her guests – Jesus and the disciples – in the best of conditions. Jesus will not reproach this obvious mark of Martha's charity. Her sister

Mary chooses to serve Jesus himself by being entirely attentive to his presence and by listening to his Word. She offers this moment, for belonging entirely to Jesus. This other expression of charity focuses directly on the Divine Person of Jesus. He compliments her by showing that the service of God must always precede the service of our neighbour, even if the two are intrinsically linked. God is served first! The two commandments of love (cf. *Mt* 22: 27-29) are applied by the two sisters. Mary loves God with all her heart, with all her soul, and with all her mind by "wasting" a little of her time on the Lord. She is the first contemplative. Martha loves her neighbours with all her strength by serving them as best she can. This is charity towards our neighbour. The double commandment finds its unity and source in the Divine Person of Jesus, at once true God and true man. Today, the Eucharist contains the Divine Person of Jesus. From this seat of charity, divine love comes to renew human love.

Prayer, as a means of drawing ever new strength from Christ, is concretely and urgently needed. People who pray are not wasting their time, even though the situation appears desperate and seems to call for action alone. Piety does not undermine the struggle against the poverty of our neighbours, however extreme. In the example of Blessed Teresa of Calcutta we have a clear illustration of the fact that time devoted to God in prayer not only does not detract from effective and loving service to our neighbour but is in fact the inexhaustible source of that service.[54]

Here are a few quotations from St Teresa of Calcutta showing the link between the two great dimensions of the commandment of charity, or of the service to be rendered to God and to men.

"You shall love the Lord your God with all your heart": "The time you spend with Jesus in the Blessed Sacrament is the best time that you can spend on earth. Each instant spent with Jesus will deepen your union with him, will make your immortal soul more glorious and more beautiful in heaven, and will contribute to bringing an eternal peace on earth." "To the question, 'What will save the world?' I respond prayer. Every parish must keep itself at the foot of Jesus in the Blessed Sacrament in hours of adoration."[55]

We should strongly support perpetual adoration with exposition. Jesus made himself the Bread of Life to give us life. Day and night, he is there. If you really want to grow in love, return to the Eucharist, return to Eucharistic adoration. We must weave our lives around the Eucharist... Fix your eyes on the One who is light; put your hearts near his Divine Heart; ask him to grant you the grace of knowing him, the love of loving him, the courage of serving him. Seek him fervently. Through Mary, the cause of our joy, you will discover that nowhere in the world are you better welcomed and nowhere in the world are you better loved than by Jesus living and truly present in the Most Blessed Sacrament… He is truly there in Person, waiting for you.[56]

"You shall love your neighbour as yourself": The Eucharist is the sacrament of love that strengthens our heart through divine charity. In the first paragraph, make note of the three quite distinct graces that St Teresa's religious sisters obtain by adoring the Blessed Sacrament daily. What is the great grace evoked in the fourth paragraph?

Each day, we expose the Blessed Sacrament, and we have perceived a change in our life. We have felt a deeper love for Christ through the distressing mask of the poor. We have been able to know ourselves better and to know the poor man better as a concrete expression of God. Since we began this adoration of the Blessed Sacrament, we have not reduced our work; we devote just as much time to it as before, but with more understanding. People accept us better. They are hungry for God. They have need, no longer of us, but of Jesus.[57]

The Eucharist is for us the sacrament of prayer, the source and summit of Christian life. The holy hour before the Eucharist must lead us to the holy hour with the poor, with those who will never have human accomplishments and for whom the sole consolation will be Jesus. Our Eucharist is incomplete if it does not lead us to the service and love of the poor. And by receiving the Communion of the poor, we discover our own poverty. That our hands must be pure in order to touch the Body of Christ, just as the priest touches it under the appearance of bread... Think of the delicacy with which the priest treats the Body of Christ during the Mass. It is this Body that you will touch in the person of the poor.[58]

When you contemplate the crucifix, you understand how much Jesus has loved you. When you contemplate the sacred Host, you understand how much Jesus loves you in this moment.[59]

Our daily hour of adoration is our family prayer where we come together before the Blessed Sacrament exposed in the monstrance. During the first half-hour, we recite the chaplet, and during the second half-hour, we pray in silence. Through our adoration, the number of our vocations has doubled. In 1963, we had one hour of adoration together each week, but it was only in 1973 when we began to do our daily hour of adoration that our community began to grow and prosper.[60]

STAGE 13

The Haemorrhaging Woman and the Act of Faith
Prolonging and Intensifying Mass

As he went, the people pressed round him. And a woman who had had a flow of blood for twelve years and had spent all her living upon physicians and could not be healed by any one, came up behind him, and touched the fringe of his garment; and immediately her flow of blood ceased. And Jesus said, "Who was it that touched me?" When all denied it, Peter said, "Master, the multitudes surround you and press upon you!" But Jesus said, "Someone touched me; for I perceive that power has gone forth from me." And when the woman saw that she was not hidden, she came trembling, and falling down before him declared in the presence of all the people why she had touched him, and how she had been immediately healed. And he said to her, "Daughter, your faith has made you well; go in peace." (*Lk* 8:42-48)

The multitudes press upon Jesus from all parts to hear him and see him perform signs and wonders. In this commotion, a woman touches Jesus with her faith, thus freeing his power. Jesus is conscious of the power that has gone forth from him and says: "Who was it that touched me?" Our faith touches the Heart of Jesus; it frees his power and his love, healing our being, our family, and the whole world, each time that we go to him in the Blessed Sacrament for an hour's adoration. Moreover, St John reminds us that "this is the victory that overcomes the world, our faith" (*1 Jn* 5:4). To the one who prays to him God gives faith. Nevertheless, it is possible to lose this inestimable gift. Paul warns Timothy of this: "Wage the good warfare, holding faith and a good conscience. By rejecting conscience, certain persons have made shipwreck of their faith" (*1 Tm* 1:18-19).

Faith is the pure act of the spirit, freed from the senses. For here (before the Blessed Sacrament), the senses are of no use; they have no part to play. It is the only mystery of Jesus Christ where the senses must be absolutely still. In all the others, in the Incarnation, the redemption, the senses see a child God, a dying God. Here, there is nothing but an impenetrable cloud for them. Faith alone must act; it is the kingdom of faith. This cloud asks of us a very meritorious sacrifice, the sacrifice of our reason and of our mind. It is necessary to believe as though against the witness of the senses, against ordinary laws of beings, against one's own experience. It is necessary to believe on the basis of the simple word of Jesus Christ; there is only one question to ask: "Who is there?" "Me", answers Jesus Christ. Let us fall to the ground and adore!

And this pure faith freed from the senses, free in its action, unites us simply to the truth of Jesus Christ in the Most Blessed Sacrament: "Faith is of no use, says the Saviour; my words are spirit and life." The soul crosses the barrier of the senses and enters into the wonderful contemplation of the divine presence of God under the species, veiled enough so that we can handle the brightness, clear enough for the eyes of faith. Much more, rather than being a trial, this veil becomes, for a humble and sincere faith, a stimulus, an encouragement.

We like to penetrate a veiled truth, to discover a hidden treasure, to overcome a difficulty. Thus the faithful soul, in the presence of the Eucharistic veil, seeks her Lord, like Magdalen at the tomb: her desire grows; she calls him like the bride of the Canticle; she pleases herself in giving him all beauties, in decorating him with all glories. The Eucharist is for her what God is for the blessed: a truth, a beauty ever ancient, ever new, that one never wearies of contemplating, of penetrating. Only our Lord's wisdom and goodness could invent the Eucharistic veil.[61]

For St Padre Pio, "It is easier for the world to survive without the sun than without the Holy Sacrifice of the Mass." If the celebration of the Mass is the centre, source, and summit of every Christian life, why, some ask, is it still necessary to adore the Blessed Sacrament? Does the Mass not contain the entire Christian mystery? What is the good of spending time in silence before the tabernacle? Certainly, nothing could supplant the Mass. Yet Eucharistic adoration is strongly encouraged by the Church. For Benedict XVI, "The act of adoration outside Mass *prolongs* and *intensifies* all that takes place during the liturgical celebration itself."[62] The two verbs "prolong" and "intensify" deserve our attention so that we can understand better why adoration is "not a luxury…but a priority"[63] in the Church today.

Prolong: "Eucharistic adoration is simply the natural consequence of the Eucharistic celebration, which is itself the Church's supreme act of adoration. Receiving the Eucharist means adoring him whom we receive."[64] Adoration of the Blessed Sacrament finds its source and foundation in the Mass. That Christians are invited to prolong their adoration after Mass does not signify that they have not participated very well at Mass. Adoration would then be a kind of second chance, a "trump card" for absent-minded Christians, inattentive during Mass. No! The mystery celebrated at Mass is prolonged in the tabernacle. Here are two analogies that can clarify our understanding, even though they are insufficient to understand the mystery: just as the ground cannot absorb all of the water that falls from the sky during a heavy rain (the Mass), this very earth continues to absorb the water by letting it seep in over a long time (adoration). We could also say that adoration is like a freeze frame because everything goes so quickly at Mass! It is Jesus's entire work of redemption, from the Incarnation to Pentecost, which is made present and unfurled before us. The Mass will always offer more than we can ever receive. So let us know how to stop and take the time to contemplate all that is made present in the Mass in the silence of adoration! "Be still, and know that I am God" (*Ps* 46:10).

Intensify: What, in the Mass, can be intensified by Eucharistic adoration? Here, we must distinguish between the gift offered by God and our disposition to receive it. The gift offered, namely, the entire work of redemption, finds its source in the Mass and is prolonged in adoration. So it is always the gift that is first at Mass. On the other hand, our interior disposition to receive this gift is directly linked to our faith. Our faith makes the gift of the Eucharist effective in us. Do we have to say that the adorer makes a more significant act of faith during his silent prayer before the Blessed Sacrament than when he participates at Mass? No, because faith is first of all made living in the liturgy of the Mass. Nevertheless, to give and adore, above all in the middle of the night, requires a different act of faith. This act is grounded in freedom, and no moral or spiritual obligation has been formulated by the Church in favour of Eucharistic adoration. We can also recognise that, during Mass, we are carried by the liturgy, while during an hour of silent adoration, we so often have occasion to ask ourselves

82

what we are doing there! So it is necessary to direct acts of faith towards the Real Presence, which strengthens our faith and obtains an abundance of Eucharistic graces for us. Kneeling before the Eucharist is truly a profession of freedom. In the end, it is the most worthwhile and radical remedy against the idolatries of yesterday and of today.

Adoring the Body of Christ, means believing that there, in that piece of Bread, Christ is really there, and gives true sense to life, to the immense universe as to the smallest creature, to the whole of human history as to the most brief existence. Adoration is prayer that prolongs the celebration and Eucharistic communion and in which the soul continues to be nourished: it is nourished with love, truth, peace; it is nourished with hope, because the One before whom we prostrate ourselves does not judge us, does not crush us but liberates and transforms us.[65]

STAGE 14

Modes of Christ's Presence
Extensions of the Incarnation

At the time of the Ascension, Jesus leaves his disciples in a paradox. What paradox? (cf. *Mt* 28:20 and *Ac* 1:9) How is it possible to leave and stay at the same time? But Jesus makes a promise. What promise (cf. *Ac* 1:8)? At the time of Pentecost, the Holy Spirit makes Jesus present to his Church in different ways. We are all called to meet Jesus in his different modes of presence each day. Connect the modes of presence and biblical verses below.

In the table on pages 84-85, link the boxes of the different columns by connecting the bullet points. Recalling these different modes of presence, Paul VI writes:

These various ways in which Christ is present fill the mind with astonishment and offer the Church a mystery for her contemplation. But there is another way in which Christ is present in his Church, a way that surpasses all the others. It is his presence in the Sacrament of the Eucharist, which is, for this reason, "a more consoling source of devotion, a lovelier object of contemplation and holier in what it contains" than all the other sacraments; for it contains Christ himself and it is "a kind of consummation of the spiritual life"... This presence is called "real" not to exclude the idea that the others are "real" too, but rather to indicate presence *par excellence*, because it is substantial and through it Christ becomes present whole and entire, God and man.[66]

Jesus extends his Incarnation to the Blessed Sacrament. All he did two thousand years ago in his natural life is prolonged for us in the sacramental mode. He wants to associate us with the mysteries of his own life. Scripture says, "Jesus Christ is the same yesterday and today and for ever" (*Heb* 13:8). In other words, he who became incarnate two thousand years ago is present today in the Eucharist in order to extend his salvation and the wonders of his love to our time. "For in this one mystery the entire supernatural order, with all its wealth and variety of wonders, is in a manner summed up and contained:... [The Eucharist] should be regarded as in a manner a continuation and extension of the Incarnation."[67]

Mode of Presence			Corresponding Biblical Verses			Biblical References
In the Church gathered together in the name of the Lord	•	•	"As you did it to one of the least of these my brethren, you did it to me."	•	•	(*Mt* 28:19) (*Jn* 20:22-23)

Mode of Presence		Corresponding Biblical Verses			Biblical References
In the Church that prays; in the heart of the baptised	• •	"For where two or three are gathered in my name, there am I in the midst of them."	• •		(Jn 6:51)
In the Church that reads the Word of God	• •	"He who receives you receives me, and he who receives me receives him who sent me."	• •		(Mt 25:40)
In the Church that acts in charity	• •	"You are God's temple... God's spirit dwells in you." "Christ may dwell in your hearts through faith."	• •		(Jn 1:1; Heb 1:1-2; Rv 1:16)
In the Church that teaches	• •	"[Baptise] them in the name of the Father and of the Son and of the Holy Spirit." "Receive the Holy Spirit. If you forgive the sins of any, they are forgiven; if you retain the sins of any, they are retained."	• •		(Mt 18:20)
In the Church that celebrates the sacraments, through priests acting "in persona Christi"	• •	Jesus, Word of God incarnate, the spoken Word of God.	• •		(Mt 10:40)
In the Eucharist	• •	"I am the living bread which came down from heaven."	• •		(1 Co 3:16) (Ep 3:17)

He will come again one day in glory, "in the same way as you saw him go into heaven" (*Ac* 1:11). He was lifted up into a cloud (*Ac* 1:9). This cloud recalls the hidden presence of God in the midst of his people (cf. *Ex* 14:19; 16:10ff.). In the Eucharist, Jesus remains in the midst of his people, in a hidden manner, to guide and protect them. One day, he will come again in his glory. Then the cloud will recede and all will see him with their eyes…

In coming before the Blessed Sacrament, we go

to Bethlehem ("house of bread"): we have the same privilege as the shepherds and the Magi come from so far to prostrate themselves before the same Jesus that we can adore in the sacred Host… Let us not pay attention to the poor state of our soul, as Mary did not pay attention to the cold and miserable state of the stable. May our spirit, like that of Mary, find its joy in God its Saviour!

to the temple: where Mary presented Jesus to the Father and consecrated him. Simeon's prophecy is realised anew: Jesus in the Eucharist is neglected and ignored. He is a stumbling block.

to Cana: just as Jesus changed water into wine, so, too, here in the Blessed Sacrament, he transforms our heart of stone into a heart of flesh, our deaths into life, and our failures into divine successes according to his words: "I will take out of your flesh the heart of stone and give you a heart of flesh" (*Ezk* 36:26). In the Blessed Sacrament, we drink from the source of living water that flows from his Heart.

to Jesus who preaches and heals: in the Blessed Sacrament, he heals us and leads us by his light. If we are ill, tired, he is the doctor. If we are sad, he gives us his joy. If we are under temptation, he gives us his peace, his strength. He awaits our response to his invitation of love, because "love is not loved!" (St Francis of Assisi). He who is rich makes himself poor to enrich us with his grace and clothe us with his glory each time we approach him in the Blessed Sacrament.

to the institution of the Eucharist: he gives us again this food for eternal life.

to Gethsemane: where he repeats: "Could you not watch one hour?" (*Mk* 14:37)

to the foot of the cross: there, the good thief is forgiven. The Blessed Sacrament is divine mercy personified. He burns with the desire to forgive. The Eucharist is the fruit of the Passion of Christ. As wheat is ground to become bread, Jesus, in his Passion, is struck, beaten, pierced through to become our living bread. He awaits our total gift, in response to the gift of himself in the Eucharist.

to the Resurrection: we are in the presence of the Resurrected One, who repeats his words: "Peace be withmyou." In the Blessed Sacrament, the power of his Resurrection pours out on those who find themselves in his presence. He sends us off to bear witness to the marvels of his love.

STAGE 15

The Shock of the Bodily Presence
of the Resurrected One

How are we to understand these words that travel down the centuries: "Where two or three are gathered in my name, there am I in the midst of them" (*Mt* 18:20)? He is there in the midst of them; he is present with a spiritual presence. In the uprightness of their hearts, the Word made flesh is present with a *spiritual presence* there where two or three are gathered in his name. But in the Eucharist, the Word made flesh is *present bodily*. Here a new dimension is added.

This bodily presence of Christ is not only when two or three are gathered in his name, so long as they are before the Blessed Sacrament. There is an important distinction to underline! By his bodily presence something like a *shock* is added to the spiritual presence of Christ.

For example, the evening in the Cenacle, the apostles are gripped by fear; they are afraid of persecution; and of whom are they thinking if not the Saviour Jesus? They have no other horizon besides him; they are all preoccupied with him and with the persecution to be undergone for him. And then, all the doors being shut, Jesus appears in his body: "Peace be with you." Suddenly, something hits them, *it is a real shock, it is the bodily presence of Christ in their midst*; this is not just anything! The bodily presence of Christ is not going to diminish the intensity of his spiritual presence.

Another example: the apostle Thomas was not there when the resurrected Jesus appeared. Thomas the apostle says: "I will not believe unless I see." Thomas is a discouraged person. He had had so much confidence in Christ that he said: "Lord, let us go and die with you." And then, everything fell apart, everything was broken; he is despairing. He is no braggart being bull-headed; no, he is crushed; "I will not believe unless I place my hand in his side." This is why Jesus comes towards him; if he had been bull-headed, Jesus would have left him to his certitude. And eight days later, Jesus comes again and says to Thomas: "Put your hand in the wound in my side and your finger in the wounds of my hands." Then, at the shock of the presence of Jesus, he falls on his knees: "My Lord and my God!"

In the resurrected Christ, there is at once a tangible certainty and the act of faith in his divinity. There is a tangible certainty: it is really he, it is his humanity that is there. So this is a historical fact, noted throughout history. The observation of the Christ's Resurrection is historical. He with whom the apostles shared their lives in Galilee, in Samaria, it is he who now is resurrected. But this historical observation of his humanity overflows, as it were, with the mystery of the glory of the resurrected Christ. Believing is necessary, believing in the divinity of Christ: "My Lord and my God!"

Some use the pretext of this language about the resurrected Christ to say that it is only a mystery and, consequently, that it was not historically manifest. But there is a historical root available, the witness of the apostles. During Christ's time of pilgrimage, it was no different: the apostles saw the humanity of Christ, but his divinity they had to believe. They had to ask for the same certainty of faith that we have to ask for today. The life of Christ, during the thirty-three years he lived in the midst of the world and the apostles, was the life of the Son of God. Consequently, he was the man whose divinity had to be believed in while grasping his humanity. And through his humanity, a kind of light made him shine in the midst of all the friends of God: "No one has spoken like this man."

So you can see how, at the Cenacle, the apostles suddenly felt the bodily presence of Christ; what richness! It is the same thing at Emmaus: Jesus speaks with them without making himself known; he tempers his glory. At Emmaus, if Christ had let out all the power of transfiguration in him, it would have been the end of the world. He himself, the disciples, and the whole world would have been transfigured. So when he appears, he is obliged to moderate the splendour of his divinity.

When we see him, it will be the transfiguration of the whole world. But even when he tempers his glory, the disciples at Emmaus divine that it is he, but they do not dare to ask him the question. They wait for a sign; it is really he who is present bodily, but not in order to continue his life of vulnerability. Something has changed in him. It is he himself in another state; so Jesus gives them a sign, the breaking of the bread. At that very moment, they have no more hesitation. They believe.

There is also the bodily presence of Jesus resurrected on the bank of the lake of Tiberias: they have fished all night and caught nothing. Then, towards morning, they notice Jesus on the shore. Immediately, the most intuitive of the apostles, the contemplative, he whom Jesus loves, says: "It is the Lord!" But he does not move; he has recognised him; he does not need to go to him because they have met through the heart. St Peter, the man of action, jumps immediately into the water; he never hesitates, St Peter, even if he is never the first to see! There again you have the appearance of Christ in the midst of them, and again it is a shock, the shock of the bodily presence of Christ in the midst of the apostles.

Do you see now what the bodily presence of the Word made flesh is going to signify for the bodily presence of Jesus in the tabernacle? That is what we have in the Eucharist.

And finally, we can meditate on the resurrection of Lazarus. At Bethany, the village of Martha and her sister, Mary, there was a sick man, Lazarus. This Mary was the one who anointed the Lord with perfume and wiped his feet with her hair. It was her brother, Lazarus, who was sick. Jesus had had to flee from Judea and go to the other side of the Jordan because his hour had not yet come; he smelled the persecution, the death that is near. So the two sisters sent a message to Jesus, saying: "Lord, he whom you love is ill." To this news, Jesus responded: "This illness is not unto death; it is for the glory of God, so that the Son of God may be glorified by means of it." Jesus loved Martha and her sister and Lazarus.

When he learned that this Lazarus was ill, he stayed two days longer in the place where he was; only then did he say to his disciples: "Let us go into Judea again." The disciples said to him: "Rabbi, the Jews were but now seeking to stone you and you are going there again?" There is a time for death and a time for life. Jesus wanted them to understand this, so he added: "Our friend Lazarus has fallen asleep, but I go to awake him out of sleep." The disciples said: "Lord, if he has fallen asleep, he will recover." Jesus had spoken of his death, but they thought he was speaking of sleep, of rest. So Jesus told them clearly: "Lazarus is dead; and for your sake I am glad that I was not there, so that you may believe." Then Jesus went to Lazarus. So Thomas, called the Twin, said to his fellow disciples: "Let us also go, that we may die with him." As I was telling you, Thomas was a generous man who had put everything on Jesus, and everything fell apart.

At his arrival, Jesus found Lazarus entombed for four days already. Bethany is only about fifteen furlongs away from Jerusalem. Many Jews had come to Martha and Mary to console them concerning their brother. When Martha learned of the arrival of Jesus, she went to meet him, while Mary remained seated in the house. And Martha said to Jesus: "Lord, if you had been here, my brother would not have died." If he had been there, would he have been able to resist the prayers of Martha and Mary? "If you had been here, my brother would not have died. And even now I know that whatever you ask from God, God will give you." With these words, she went to call her sister, Mary, and she said to her quietly: "The Teacher is here and is calling for you." Mary, at this news, rose quickly and went to him. Jesus had not yet entered the village; he was at the place where Martha had met him. When the Jews, who were with Mary in the house consoling her, saw her rise quickly and go out, they followed her, thinking that she was going to the tomb to weep there. When she came to the place where Jesus was, as soon as she saw him, she fell at his feet and said to him: "Lord, if you had been here, my brother would not have died" (cf. *Jn* 11).

Do you see now what the bodily presence of Jesus is? "If you had been here…" There are, then, things he grants when we are gathered for and in the Eucharist and that he does not grant whenever two or three are gathered in his name, where there is simply the spiritual presence. The spiritual presence is an immense dimension, but there is more; there is the bodily presence of the Word made flesh. The bodily presence of Christ in glory is there in the most humble of our chapels, waiting. And in a sense it remains true to say that he is there in agony until the end of the world, in the heart of the tempests of history, and that we must not sleep during this time. Must the complaint still be made to us: "So, could you not watch with me one hour?" (*Mt* 26:40).

    – Cardinal Journet[68]

THE SIGNS OF THE COVENANT

STAGE 16
Covenants in the Bible

After having meditated on the love of Jesus in the Eucharist and on his desire to be loved (cf. *first fifteen stages*), in this new phase, we follow some of the great biblical passages concerning the signs of the Covenant, or the sacraments. We will study how these passages are centred on the Eucharist and how we can be nourished from it through faith.

In these verses, find each one of the Persons of the Trinity at work in creation:

> In the beginning God created the heavens and the earth. The earth was without form and void, and darkness was upon the face of the deep; and the Spirit [wind] of God was moving over the face of the waters. And God said, "Let there be light"; and there was light. (*Gn* 1:1-3)

"God" is the Father; the "wind" indicates the Holy Spirit; "God said" indicates the Word, the speech of the Father (cf. *Jn* 1:1). God is not solitary, he is familial. He brings about the creation in order to share his life and joy.

The first story of creation (cf. *Gn* 1:1-2, 4) makes no claim to be a scientific text. This sacred text does not explain the "how" of creation, but the "why". Creation is presented as a dwelling that God carefully organises. The numbered succession of days evokes a great liturgy that is realised in the Covenant of God with men. Days 1, 2 and 3 are similar to the exterior parts of a great dwelling (foundations, walls, frame of the roof). What is created during days 4, 5 and 6 is put in the interior of the dwelling. The story does not end with the creation of man and woman. On the seventh day, God "rests". The final end of creation, this day is the day of the Covenant when God comes to visit the first family with whom he wants to make a covenant.

Day 1: Light and darkness

Day 2: Firmament [69] (water from the heavens and from the earth)

Day 3: Land and vegetation

Day 4: Celestial bodies (sun, moon, stars)

Day 5: Birds, fish

Day 6: Animals and men/women (image of God)

Day 7: God's rest: Time of the Covenant

The Covenant, dwelling of God in the midst of his people: "And I will make my abode among you, and my soul shall not abhor you. And I will walk among you, and will be your God, and you shall be my people" (*Lv* 26:11-12). According to Leviticus 26, what is a covenant? How does a covenant involve God? How does it involve man? What is the difference between a contract and a covenant? What is given in a contract? In a covenant? For how long? Covenants involve the person, the heart, for life.

> God, infinitely perfect and blessed in himself, in a plan of sheer goodness freely created man to make him share in his own blessed life. For this reason, at every time and in every place, God draws close to man. He calls man to seek him, to know him, to love him with all his strength. He calls together all men, scattered and divided by sin, into the unity of his family, the Church. To accomplish this, when the fullness of time had come, God sent his Son as Redeemer and Saviour. In his Son and through him, he invites men to become, in the Holy Spirit, his adopted children and thus heirs of his blessed life.[70]

Throughout the whole of sacred history, God comes to live with his people. He was present during the Exodus in the tent of meeting, then at Jerusalem in the temple of Solomon. He came to live among us by taking a body: "Consequently, when Christ came into the world, he said, 'Sacrifices and offerings you have not desired, but a body have you prepared for me'" (*Heb* 10:5). Or again: "The Word became flesh and dwelt among us" (*Jn* 1:14), literally: "He pitched his tent among us." At the end of his life on earth, the Heart of Jesus invents the Eucharist to continue to dwell in the midst of his people until the end of the world because the Shepherd does not abandon his flock with the passing of time. Pope St John Paul II explained: "The Lord Jesus has pitched his tent among us and, from this his Eucharistic dwelling, he repeats to each man and each woman, 'Come to me, all you who labour and are overburdened, and I shall give you rest'" (*Mt* 11:28). [71]

Let us look more closely at the first five covenants in the Old Testament and the new and eternal Covenant sealed in the Eucharist, presented in the New Testament:

> God said, "Let us make man in our image, after our likeness…" So God created man in his own image, in the image of God he created him; male and female he created them. And God blessed them, and God said to them, "Be fruitful and multiply, and fill the earth and subdue it; and have dominion over the fish of the sea and over the birds of the air and over every living thing that moves upon the earth" (*Gn* 1:26-28).

Here we have the first covenant with a couple. The couple is called to co-operate with the plan of God in the gift of life. While reading the following texts, find what God promises in each of the covenants. With whom does God conclude them? A family (Adam and Eve), three families (Noah), a clan or tribe (Abraham), twelve tribes (Moses), an empire (David). Note the numerical progression of the persons implicated in each of the covenants. Towards what are we progressing?

"But I will establish my covenant with you; and you shall come into the ark, you, your sons, your wife, and your sons' wives with you." (*Gn* 6:18)

God said, "This is the sign of the covenant... I set my bow in the cloud, and it shall be a sign of the covenant between me and the earth. When I bring clouds over the earth and the bow is seen in the clouds, I will remember my covenant which is between me and you and every living creature of all flesh; and the waters shall never again become a flood to destroy all flesh." (*Gn* 9:12-15)

When Abram was ninety-nine years old, the Lord appeared to Abram, and said to him, "I am God Almighty; walk before me, and be blameless..." Then Abram fell on his face; and God said to him, "Behold, my covenant is with you, and you shall be the father of a multitude of nations. No longer shall your name be Abram, but your name shall be Abraham; for I have made you the father of a multitude of nations. I will make you exceedingly fruitful; and I will make nations of you, and kings shall come forth from you. And I will establish my covenant between me and you and your descendants after you throughout their generations for an everlasting covenant, to be God to you and to your descendants after you. And I will give to you, and to your descendants after you, the land of your sojournings, all the land of Canaan, for an everlasting possession; and I will be their God." (*Gn* 17:1, 3-8)

The Lord said to Moses, "Write these words; in accordance with these words I have made a covenant with you and with Israel." And he was there with the Lord forty days and forty nights; he neither ate bread nor drank water. And he wrote upon the tables the words of the covenant, the Ten Commandments. (*Ex* 34:27-28)

God addresses David through the intermediary of the prophet Nathan:

"When your days are fulfilled and you lie down with your fathers, I will raise up your offspring after you, who shall come forth from your body, and I will establish his kingdom. He shall build a house for my name, and I will establish the throne of his kingdom for ever. I will be his father, and he shall be my son… And your house and your kingdom shall be made sure for ever before me; your throne shall be established for ever." (*2 S* 7:12-14, 16)

This text presents the Covenant with David and his dynasty. As the Jerusalem Bible notes, the prophecy is constructed around an opposition: it is not David who will make a *house* (a temple) for the Lord, but it is the Lord who will make a *house* (a dynasty) for David.

Now as they were eating, Jesus took bread, and blessed, and broke it, and gave it to the disciples and said, "Take, eat; this is my body." And he took a chalice, and when he had given thanks he gave it to them, saying, "Drink of it,

all of you; for this is my blood of the covenant, which is poured out for many for the forgiveness of sins."
(*Mt* 26:26-28)

With whom does God conclude the New Covenant? In the Old Testament, God concluded covenants with his people. What do we call the new people of God? How does this people, the Church, come into being? The Church is the Body of Christ. As Pseudo-Jerome affirms, "The Eucharist makes the Church, and the Church makes the Eucharist."

St Augustine develops this idea:

This bread that you see on the altar, once sanctified by the Word of God, is the Body of Christ. This cup, or rather the drink it contains, once sanctified by the Word of God, is the Blood of Christ. Our Lord Jesus Christ wanted to bestow here his Body and Blood, which he shed for us in remission of sins. If you have received them well, you are yourself what you have received.[72]

Consequently, "we have become not only Christians, but Christ himself."[73] "Christ is not in the head without being in the body, Christ is entirely in the head and in the body."[74]

The Eucharist, as the sacrifice of the New Covenant, is the development and fulfilment of the covenant celebrated on Sinai when Moses poured half the blood of the sacrificial victims on the altar, the symbol of God, and half on the assembly of the children of Israel (cf. *Ex* 24:5-8). This "blood of the covenant" closely united God and man in a bond of solidarity. With the Eucharist the intimacy becomes total; the embrace between God and man reaches its apex. This is the fulfilment of that "new covenant" which Jeremiah had foretold (cf. 31:31-34): a pact in the spirit and in the heart, which the Letter to the Hebrews extols precisely by taking the prophet's oracle and linking it to Christ's one definitive sacrifice (cf. *Heb* 10:14-17).[75]

STAGE 17
The Memorial

The Lord said to Moses and Aaron in the land of Egypt, "This month shall be for you the beginning of months; it shall be the first month of the year for you. Tell all the congregation of Israel that on the tenth day of this month they shall take every man a lamb according to their fathers' houses, a lamb for a household... This day shall be for you a memorial day, and you shall keep it as a feast to the Lord; throughout your generations you shall observe it as an ordinance for ever." (*Ex* 12:1-3, 14)

At each benediction of the Blessed Sacrament, the priest prays like this:

Lord Jesus Christ, you gave us the Eucharist as *the memorial of suffering and death.* May our worship of this sacrament of your body and blood help us to experience the salvation you won for us and the peace of the kingdom where you live with the Father and the Holy Spirit for ever and ever. Amen.

The Eucharist is the memorial of the suffering and death of Christ. In the Bible and the liturgy, the memorial is not only a memory or a place of memory as we hear it said today. The memorial comprises three distinct dimensions:

• First *it recalls the liberating action* of God for his people. "Remember this day, in which you came out from Egypt, out of the house of bondage, for by the strength of hand the Lord brought you out from this place" (*Ex* 13:3).

• Next, the memorial makes present and effective for his people what God has done in the past. Thus, each year, the people of Israel celebrated the Passover (cf. *Ex* 12:25-27), *making present the salvation of God* from the new forms of slavery suffered by Israel.

• Lastly, the memorial anticipates the Day of the Lord, that is, the total and definitive liberation from all evil, from all bondage, and from death, when at the end of time, all things will be subjected to God and he will be everything to everyone (cf. *1 Co* 15:28).

In the Bible, celebrating the Passover is remembering the wonders of God. In the verses from St Luke below, find first what belongs to the ancient rite (the Jewish Passover that Jesus celebrates in the Jewish tradition, the memorial of God's liberation of his people). Then find what belongs to the new rite of the Christian Eucharist, the memorial of his Passion, celebrated at each Mass.

[The disciples] prepared the Passover. And when the hour came, he sat at table and the apostles with him. And he said to them, "I have earnestly desired to eat this Passover with you before I suffer; for I tell you I shall not eat it until it is fulfilled in the kingdom of God." And he took a chalice, and when he had given thanks he said, "Take this, and divide it among yourselves; for I tell you that from now on I shall not drink of the fruit of the vine until the kingdom of God comes."

And he took bread, and when he had given thanks he broke it and gave it to them, saying, "This is my body which is given for you. Do this in remembrance of me." And likewise the chalice after supper, saying, "This chalice which is poured out for you is the new covenant in my blood." (*Lk* 22:13-20)

The Jewish Passover was the memorial of God's action of liberation from the political slavery of Pharaoh. But Jesus came to free man from another form of slavery. Since it is not from political servitude (cf. *Jn* 6:15), what is this slavery of which man is at once victim and guilty? And what is its direct consequence for man? "The wages of sin is death" (*Rm* 6:23). The word "Passover" recalls "passage". To what passage of the Jewish people does this refer? What is the Passover (the passage) of Jesus? And for us, what is our Passover? "If the Spirit of him who raised Jesus from the dead dwells in you, he who raised Christ Jesus from the dead will give life to your mortal bodies also through his Spirit who dwells in you" (*Rm* 8:11).

Thus, in prolonging the Jewish Passover, Jesus celebrates the new Passover that fully accomplishes what the old one could not achieve: "When Christ appeared as a high priest of the good things that have come, then through the greater and more perfect tent (not made with hands, that is, not of this creation) he entered once for all into the Holy Place, taking not the blood of goats and calves but his own blood, thus securing an eternal redemption" (*Heb* 9:11-12).

Jesus, celebrating his Passover, leaves us the Eucharist, the memorial of his Passion. In the verses of St Paul, find the three dimensions of the memorial celebrated at each Eucharist:

> For I received from the Lord what I also delivered to you, that the Lord Jesus on the night when he was betrayed took bread, and when he had given thanks, he broke it, and said, "This is my body which is for you. Do this in remembrance of me." In the same way also the chalice, after supper, saying, "This chalice is the new covenant in my blood. Do this, as often as you drink it, in remembrance of me." For as often as you eat this bread and drink the chalice, you proclaim the Lord's death until he comes. (*1 Co* 11:23-26)

Through the Mass, the Church responds to the explicit request of Jesus, at the time of his Last Supper, to celebrate his Passover in his memory. The *anamnesis* (Greek for "memorial") proclaimed by the assembly just after the Consecration, recalls the three dimensions of the memorial precisely, according to the following traditional formulas:

The mystery of faith: We proclaim your death, O Lord, and profess your Resurrection, until you come again.

The mystery of faith: When we eat this bread and drink this cup, we proclaim your death, O Lord, until you come again.

The mystery of faith: Save us, Saviour of the world, for by your cross and Resurrection you have set us free.

A remark on the Blood of Christ, shed upon those who approach the Eucharist in faith:

After having given the Decalogue as the foundation of the Covenant between God and the people, Moses sacrifices an animal. With the blood, he sprinkles one part on the altar from which God receives the offering and the other part on the people. The aim of this gesture is to confirm the Covenant: "And Moses took the blood and threw it upon the people, and said, 'Behold the blood of the covenant which the Lord has made with you in accordance with all these words'" (*Ex* 24:8). In Matthew 27:25 and in John 11:50, find the two Gospel passages where the Blood of Jesus is called upon the people so that all may live. What passages are these? The characters who call for the Blood of Christ upon themselves act with hate, ignorance, or jealousy. It is for this reason that Christ died for all. He came to save all sinners through the New Covenant in his Blood. The Blood spilled upon the cross is made present in the Eucharist. "This is the chalice of my Blood...poured out...for many." Each time the Host is elevated or adored during the Mass, Jesus mystically sheds his Blood which saves, heals, and liberates upon all of mankind.

Anima Christi

Soul of Christ, sanctify me.
    Body of Christ, save me.
Blood of Christ, inebriate me.
Water from the side of Christ, wash me.
    Passion of Christ, strengthen me.
O good Jesus, hear me.
    Within thy wounds, hide me.
Suffer me not to be separated from thee.
    From the malignant enemy defend me.
In the hour of my death call me.
    And bid me to come to thee,
That with thy Saints I may praise thee,
    for ever and ever. Amen.[76]

STAGE 18

The Holy Sacrifice of the Mass

The Lord said to Moses and Aaron in the land of Egypt, "This month shall be for you the beginning of months; it shall be the first month of the year for you. Tell all the congregation of Israel that on the tenth day of this month they shall take every man a lamb according to their fathers' houses, a lamb for a household… Your lamb shall be without blemish, a male a year old; you shall take it from the sheep or from the goats; and you shall keep it until the fourteenth day of this month, when the whole assembly of the congregation of Israel shall kill their lambs in the evening. Then they shall take some of the blood, and put it on the two doorposts and the lintel of the houses in which they eat them. They shall eat the flesh that night, roasted; with unleavened bread and bitter herbs they shall eat it… In this manner you shall eat it: your loins girded, your sandals on your feet, and your staff in your hand; and you shall eat it in haste. It is the Lord's Passover. For I will pass through the land of Egypt that night, and I will strike all the first-born in the land of Egypt, both man and beast; and on all the gods of Egypt I will execute judgements; I am the

Lord. The blood shall be a sign for you, upon the houses where you are; and when I see the blood, I will pass over you, and no plague shall fall upon you to destroy you, when I strike the land of Egypt. This day shall be for you a memorial day, and you shall keep it as a feast to the Lord; throughout your generations you shall observe it as an ordinance for ever." (*Ex* 12:1-3, 5-8, 11-14)

In the Jewish calendar, the first month of the year is Nisan, which corresponds to March-April in our calendar. This is the month when the people of Israel celebrate their Passover. Starting with the text above, find the links between the Jewish Passover, the Passover of Jesus, and the Christian Passover, celebrated at each Mass and culminating at the Paschal Vigil.

Jewish Passover (Ex 12)	Passover of Jesus (Passion)	Christian Passover (Mass)
First month of the year (Nisan)	During the Jewish Passover	March-April: beginning of the Paschal season; new Paschal candle
Male yearling without blemish	Jesus, unstained victim (Heb 7:26), Paschal Lamb	In the sacred Host, it is the Lamb of God who takes away the sin of the world
Throat slit at twilight	Jesus expiring at the ninth hour	Paschal Vigil at twilight
Blood spilled on the lintels (protection against death)	Christ saves us by his blood (1 Jn 2:2)	The Blood of Christ shed in the Eucharist: "who eats my flesh and drinks my blood has eternal life" (Jn 6:54)
The blood is a sign (Ex 12:13)	The cross of Jesus	The appearances of bread are a sign
Flesh roasted over a fire	Sufferings and sacrifice of Christ on the cross	The Mass makes present the sacrifice of Christ
Your loins girded, your sandals on your feet: passage from slavery to freedom	Christ descends into death and opens the gates of heaven	The Eucharist is the sacrament of eternal life

The Passover of the Jews was at hand, and Jesus went up to Jerusalem. In the temple he found those who were selling oxen and sheep and pigeons, and the money-changers at their business. And making a whip of cords, he drove them all, with the sheep and oxen, out of the temple; and he poured out the coins of the money-changers and overturned their tables. And he told those who sold the pigeons, "Take these things away; you shall not make my Father's house a house of trade." His disciples remembered that it was written, "Zeal for your house will consume me." The Jews then said to him, "What sign have you to show us for doing this?" Jesus answered them, "Destroy this temple, and in three days I will raise it up." The Jews then said, "It has taken forty-six years to build this temple, and will you raise it up in three days?" But he spoke of the temple of his body. When therefore he was raised from the dead, his disciples remembered that he had said this; and they believed the Scripture and the word which Jesus had spoken. (*Jn* 2:13-22)

Jesus enters the temple for the Passover and drives away the animals that were sold for sacrifice. By this gesture, Jesus signifies that he is himself the true Lamb, who offers itself freely in sacrifice, accomplishing what the blood of the animals could not: "But when Christ appeared as a high priest of the good things that have come, then through the greater and more perfect tent (not made with hands, that is, not of this creation) he entered once for all into the Holy Place, taking not the blood of goats and calves but his own blood, thus securing an eternal redemption" (*Heb* 9:11-12).

"Destroy this temple, and in three days I will raise it up": the temple is the place where God dwells in the midst of his people. Of what temple is Jesus speaking? Here is the testimony of John the Baptist at the Jordan: "I saw the Spirit descend as a dove from heaven and remain on him" (*Jn* 1:32). At what time will this temple be destroyed and then raised up again? As wheat is ground to become bread, the Body of Jesus is whipped, thrashed, pierced by the spear, and ground by hate, to become the living bread come down from heaven that gives life to the world (*Jn* 6:51). What then is the fruit of the Passion? How should we respond today to this prayer – "Zeal for your house will consume me" – in relation to the Eucharist, the Body of Christ that is given, and the new temple (or house) of God among men?

> And he took bread, and when he had given thanks he broke it and gave it to them, saying, "This is my body which is given for you. Do this in remembrance of me." And likewise the chalice after supper, saying, "This chalice which is poured out for you is the new covenant in my blood" (*Lk* 22:19-20).

This passage makes clear the sacrificial character of the Eucharist. What are the two verbs that Jesus uses to express the offering that he makes of his Body and Blood? These verbs must be understood in their literal sense. Given, that is, sacrificed; poured out, that is, shed unto death. "Body", in Semitic languages, recalls the person, with all he has done, said, and been throughout his life. "Blood" is the seat of life (cf. *Gn* 9:4). During the Last Supper, Jesus gives his blood separately from the body. This anticipates his death. In giving over his body and his blood, Jesus gives all he has, all he is, his life and his death. His offering is total. In commanding his apostles: "Do this in remembrance of me", Jesus makes of the Eucharistic celebration a sacrifice. The Mass is the unbloody representation of the bloody sacrifice of Jesus on the cross. It makes present and effective the fruit of redemption for the Church and for the world.

In the text below, Benedict XVI shows how the Mass is a sacrifice that saves the world. Find in this text the four great transformations worked by Christ. What is their source?

In their hearts, people always and everywhere have somehow expected a change, a transformation of the world. Here now is the central act of transformation that alone can truly renew the world: violence is transformed into love, and death into life. Since this act transmutes death into love, death as such is already conquered from within, the Resurrection is already present in it. Death is, so to speak, mortally wounded, so that it can no longer have the last word. To use an image well known to us today, this is like inducing nuclear fission in the very heart of being – the victory of love over hatred, the victory of love over death. Only this intimate explosion of good conquering evil can then trigger off the series of transformations that little by little will change the world. All other changes remain superficial and cannot save. For this reason we speak of redemption: what had to happen at the most intimate level has indeed happened, and we can enter into its dynamic. Jesus can distribute his Body, because he truly gives himself. This first fundamental transformation of violence into love, of death into life, brings other changes in its wake. Bread and wine become his Body and Blood. But it must not stop there; on the contrary, the process of transformation must now gather momentum. The Body and Blood of Christ are given to us so that we ourselves will be transformed in our turn. We are to become the Body of Christ, his own Flesh and Blood. We all eat the one bread, and this means that we ourselves become one. In this way, adoration, as we said earlier, becomes union. God no longer simply stands before us as the One who is totally Other. He is within us, and we are in him. His dynamic enters into us and then seeks to spread outward to others until it fills the world, so that his love can truly become the dominant measure of the world.[77]

A related question: Can we speak of several "offerings" of the redemptive sacrifice? "Melchizedek king of Salem brought out bread and wine; he was priest of God Most High. And he blessed him and said, 'Blessed be Abram by God Most High, maker of heaven and earth'" (*Gn* 14:18-19).

The word offering has two meanings. It can designate the sacrificial rite that makes present for us the one Sacrifice. So each Mass celebrated throughout time in fidelity to the commandment called for by Christ, "Do this in remembrance of me", is a new offering of his sacrifice. And it can signify the sacrificial act of Christ offering himself "with loud cries and tears" and becoming "the source of eternal salvation to all who obey him" (*Heb* 5:7, 9). And so all Masses refer us back to the one redemptive Offering. The enveloping offering is renewed, the enveloped offering remains unchanged.[78]

STAGE 19

The Paschal Lamb
Behold the Lamb of God

[God] said, "Take your son, your only-begotten son Isaac, whom you love, and go to the land of Moriah, and offer him there as a burnt offering upon one of the mountains of which I shall tell you." So Abraham rose early in the morning, saddled his donkey, and took two of his young men with him, and his son Isaac; and… went to the place of which God had told him… And Abraham took the wood of the burnt offering, and laid it on Isaac his son; and he took in his hand the fire and the knife. So they went both of them together. And Isaac said to his father Abraham, "My father!" And he said, "Here am I, my son." He said, "Behold, the fire and the wood; but where is the lamb for a burnt offering?" And Abraham said, "God will provide himself the lamb for a burnt offering, my son." So they went both of them together. When they came to the place of which God had told him, Abraham built an altar there, and laid the wood in order, and bound Isaac his son, and laid him on the altar, upon the wood.

Then Abraham put forth his hand, and took the knife to slay his son. But the angel of the Lord called to him from heaven, and said, "Abraham, Abraham!" And he said, "Here am I." He said, "Do not lay your hand on the lad or do anything to him; for now I know that you fear God, seeing you have not withheld your son, your only-begotten son, from me." And Abraham lifted up his eyes and looked, and behold, behind him was a ram, caught in a thicket by his horns; and Abraham went and took the ram, and offered it up as a burnt offering instead of his son. So Abraham called the name of that place The Lord will provide; as it is said to this day, "On the mount of the Lord it shall be provided."

And the angel of the Lord called to Abraham a second time from heaven, and said, "By myself I have sworn, says the Lord, because you have done this, and have not withheld your son, your only-begotten son, I will indeed bless you, and I will multiply your descendants as the stars of heaven and as the sand which is on the seashore. And your descendants shall possess the gate of their enemies, and by your descendants shall all the nations of the earth bless themselves, because you have obeyed my voice." (*Gn* 22:2-3, 6-18)

What is Isaac's dramatic question to his father Abraham? It is in fact the question that dwells in the heart of every man: What must be done to have eternal life? By what offering can I avoid death? Who will die in my place so that I may live? Isaac's question about the lamb that must be sacrificed finds no answer in the Old Testament, "for it is impossible that the blood of bulls and goats should take away sins" (*Heb* 10:4). Abraham responds mysteriously to Isaac: "God will provide." In other words, God will give the Lamb when the time is come.

> This took place in Bethany beyond the Jordan, where John was baptising... He saw Jesus coming towards him, and said, "Behold, the Lamb of God, who takes away the sin of the world!"... John bore witness, "I saw the Spirit descend as a dove from heaven and remain on him" (*Jn* 1:28-29, 32).

Thus it is John the Baptist who "answers" Isaac's great question – two thousand years later. He points out Jesus as the Lamb of God, who takes away the sin of the world. John the Baptist's term "behold" must be understood as the fulfilment of a hopeful expectation: "He is here at last."

"And when he came up out of the water, immediately he saw the heavens opened and the Spirit descending upon him like a dove; and a voice came from heaven, 'You are my beloved Son; with you I am well pleased'" (*Mk* 1:10-11). To evangelise is to announce the Good News. Jesus is the Good News. He alone can take away the sin of man and fill his heart. Thus John the Baptist is evangelised by God when he sees the Spirit descending upon Jesus and when he hears the Father point out the Son so that all may go to him. In his turn, John the Baptist will invite the crowds to follow

Jesus the Christ, he who is the true Lamb, who will die for the sins of the world. This is the Father's evangelisation, taken up by John the Baptist, the evangelisation that we in turn must continue: announcing Jesus, he who comes to free us from sin and fill us with his life-giving Spirit.

The following passage brings out the link between "adoration" and "mission" with the verbs "look" and "say". In order to announce, it is first necessary to contemplate:

> "He *looked* at Jesus as he walked, and *said*, 'Behold, the Lamb of God!' The two disciples heard him say this, and they followed Jesus. Jesus turned, and saw them following, and said to them, 'What do you seek?' And they said to him, 'Rabbi' (which means Teacher), 'where are you staying?' He said to them, 'Come and see.' They came and saw where he was staying; and they stayed with him that day, for it was about the tenth hour" (*Jn* 1:36-39).

Thanks to John the Baptist's evangelisation, two of his disciples follow Jesus. What question do they ask Jesus? As with Abraham's response to Isaac, Jesus's response will be understood later. He tells them only: "Come and see." In other words, you are going to see what you are looking for if you come follow me. Yet St John gives a major detail: it was about the tenth hour.

"It was now about the sixth hour, and there was darkness over the whole land until the ninth hour" (*Lk* 23:44).

"When they came to Jesus and saw that he was already dead, they did not break his legs. But one of the soldiers pierced his side with a spear, and at once there came out blood and water" (*Jn* 19:33-34).

Jesus is crucified at the sixth hour; he dies at the ninth. About the tenth hour, his Heart is pierced! This is where Jesus invites his disciples. He invites them to contemplate his Heart, this Heart which expresses the love of God, this Heart which, receiving hate, gives only love in response. The whole mystery of our God of love is revealed when Christ is nailed to the cross with his open Heart, from which flows water and blood. It is the birth of the Church and the sacraments. It is the place of encounter between God and mankind. This encounter is made through the infinite mercy in the Heart of God revealed at the tenth hour.

Thus, the episode of the sacrifice of Isaac makes sense in light of the baptism of Jesus, which in turn makes sense in light of the open Heart of Christ on the cross. Let us note other links between these three texts:

1. Mount Moriah, the place where Abraham goes to sacrifice Isaac, is in Jerusalem. "Then Solomon began to build the house of the Lord in Jerusalem on Mount Moriah, where the Lord had appeared to David his father" (*2 Ch* 3:1). In the centre of the temple in Jerusalem was the "Holy of Holies", the place where God dwelled among his people. It was there that the people went to adore God. It was there

that they offered sacrifices to ask forgiveness for their sins. It was at this same place that Jesus would be sacrificed, offering his life for the forgiveness of sins and revealing, through his pierced Heart, the love of God our Father.

2. Isaac carries the wood for the sacrifice in Genesis 22. He prefigures Christ, who will carry his cross during his Passion.

3. The ram, sacrificed by Abraham in place of Isaac, is caught by his horns in a bush of thorns. What link can be found with Jesus on the cross?

4. What does the following verse about Abraham's love for Isaac reveal? "Take your son, your only-begotten son Isaac, whom you love, and go to the land of Moriah, and offer him there as a burnt offering upon one of the mountains." What conclusion can be drawn about the Father's love for his Son Jesus, who will really be sacrificed and not spared, so that every person may live eternally? What can be deduced about God's love for us (cf. *Jn* 15:9)?

5. What sort of blessing does God promise Abraham because of his faith? What blessings will the Father grant to all generations who believe that Jesus died for their sins?

Thus, John the Baptist answers Isaac's question – "Where is the lamb for a burnt offering?" – by pointing out Jesus and declaring: "Behold, the Lamb of God who takes away the sin of the world." These words of the forerunner are taken up again by each priest at the elevation of the Host for the adoration of all. In the sacred Host, the Lamb of God takes away our sins by pouring out divine mercy on us and on the world. He comes to fill our heart with Holy Communion. Through Mass and adoration, the Lord gives his open Heart in the Eucharist. There, we draw abundantly from the living sources of salvation.

> "The sacrifice of Christ and the sacrifice of the Eucharist are *one single sacrifice*" [CCC 1367]. St John Chrysostom put it well: "We always offer the same Lamb, not one today and another tomorrow, but always the same one. For this reason the sacrifice is always only one... Even now we offer that victim who was once offered and who will never be consumed."[79]

Mother Marie-Thérèse Dubouché (1809-1863) wrote, when founding the Congregation of the Adoration of Reparation:

> Human misery! The way is sought everywhere: we question science, read lengthy books, consult experience, observe, reflect, consider the creature in the physical and moral orders, all of this in search of life! And the principle of life is here, he is available to us, and we disdain him to go drink from all these streams that cannot quench our thirst! How sad it is to see men who move about in vain to discover the means offending God, when they have him so close to them in this divine sacrament![80]

STAGE 20

Divine Mercy

The book of Hosea shows God's infinite mercy. The etymology of the Latin word for mercy, *misericordia*, contains two words: *miseria* (misery) and *cor* (heart). It is God who loves what is not lovable in man. Mankind's only hope, mercy, is the expression of God's love that comes to love and save what is wounded in man. What attracts God to man is not first of all his fine qualities or his virtues, but his wounds and his sin. Our good qualities are due to the new man, saved by grace. Our vices are due to the old man in us, not yet saved, but calling out for divine mercy.

God asks Hosea to take a prostitute for his wife. She continues her infidelities with her husband. Despite everything, Hosea remains faithful to her. By analogy, this story exalts the faithfulness of God, the Bridegroom, who never rejects his bride, Israel, despite her numerous infidelities. The marriage between God and his people is realised through the Covenant. So often the people will reject the Covenant with their God by worshipping other gods, the Baals. God reproaches his people for carrying on like Hosea's ungrateful bride by neglecting the Covenant and forgetting that the Covenant is the source of all goods and blessings. The first paragraph of the text sets out the list of the bride's infidelities and the just condemnation merited. We await the sentence, but instead God applies mercy. This is how God treats his children.

"Plead with your mother, plead – for she is not my wife, and I am not her husband… Therefore I will hedge up her way with thorns; and I will build a wall against her, so that she cannot find her paths. She shall pursue her lovers, but not overtake them; and she shall seek them, but shall not find them. Then she shall say, 'I will go and return to my first husband, for it was better with me then than now.' And she did not know that it was I who gave her the grain, the wine, and the oil, and who lavished upon her silver and gold which they used for Baal. Therefore I will take back my grain in its time, and my wine in its season; and I will take away my wool and my flax, which were to cover her nakedness. Now I will uncover her lewdness in the sight of her lovers, and no one shall rescue her out of my hand. And I will put an end to all her mirth, her feasts, her new moons, her Sabbaths, and all her appointed feasts. And I will lay waste her vines and her fig trees, of which she said, 'These are my hire, which my lovers have given me.' I will make them a forest, and the beasts of the field shall devour them. And I will punish her for the feast days of the Baals when she burned incense to them and decked herself with her ring and jewellery, and went after her lovers, and forgot me, says the Lord.

"*Therefore*, behold, I will allure her, and bring her into the wilderness, and speak tenderly to her. And there I will give her vineyards, and make the Valley of Achor a door of hope. And there she shall answer as in the days of her youth, as at the time when she came out of the land of Egypt. And in that day, says the Lord, you will call me, 'My husband,' and no longer will you call me, 'My Baal.' For I will remove the names of the Baals from her mouth, and they shall be mentioned by name no more. And I will make for you a covenant on that day with the beasts of the field, the birds of the air, and the creeping things of the ground; and I will abolish the bow, the sword, and war from the land; and I will make you lie down in safety. And I will espouse you for ever; I will espouse you in righteousness and in justice, in steadfast love, and in mercy." (*Ho* 2:2, 6-19)

The passage above is structured around the adverb "therefore". Rather than justly condemning, God gives proof of his mercy. Unceasingly, despite everything, he continues to love his bride, his people with whom he sealed a covenant in the desert. God's faithfulness to his people rests, not on Israel's response, but on God's promise. This is how Jesus acts in the Eucharist, the sacrament of the New Covenant. Whatever our infidelities, our ingratitude, our coldness, the Heart of Jesus would never be able to condemn, but continues to pursue us with his mercy. "How can I give you up, O Ephraim! How can I hand you over, O Israel!… My heart recoils within me, my compassion grows warm and tender" (*Ho* 11:8).

God's mercy shows itself in the book of Hosea through the words noted in the left-hand column on pages 128–130. The right-hand column sets out how this same mercy is realised today in the Eucharist (see the table on the following pages).

When leaving his parish, a holy priest, whose difficult character his parishioners knew well, gave this account: "All you have loved in me comes from the time I spent in front of the Blessed Sacrament. All that has disappointed you in me comes from the time I should have spent in front of the Blessed Sacrament."

128

Mercy in Hosea	Mercy in the Eucharist
I will allure her	He hides his divine and bodily glory so as not to dazzle and blind you. He veils his majesty so that you might dare go to him and speak to him as a friend speaks to his friend; he even tempers the ardour of his Heart and his love for you, because you could not withstand its strength and tenderness; he lets you see only that goodness which leaks out and escapes through the sacred species, like rays of the sun through a light cloud.[81]
I will bring her into the wilderness	Faith is the pure act of the spirit, freed from the senses. For here (before the Blessed Sacrament), the senses are of no use; they have no part to play. It is the only mystery of Jesus Christ where the senses must be absolutely still. In all the others, in the Incarnation, the redemption, the senses see a child God, a dying God. Here, there is nothing but an impenetrable cloud for them. Faith alone must act; it is the kingdom of faith. This cloud asks of us a very meritorious sacrifice, the sacrifice of our reason and of our mind. It is necessary to believe as though against the witness of the senses, against ordinary laws of beings, against one's own experience. It is necessary to believe on the basis of the simple word of Jesus Christ; there is only one question to ask: "Who is there?" "I am", answers Jesus Christ. Let us fall to the ground and adore![82]

Mercy in Hosea	Mercy in the Eucharist
I will speak tenderly to her; I will give her vineyards; I will be a door of hope	Our Lord, to maintain and make more effective in us the hope of heaven, to make us patiently await heaven and glory and lead us there, created the beautiful heaven of the Eucharist. For the Eucharist is a beautiful heaven, heaven begun. Is it not Jesus in glory coming from heaven to "earth" and bringing heaven with him? He comes and remains bodily in our hearts as long as the Sacrament lasts; then, the species having been destroyed, he goes up again to heaven, but remains in us through his grace and through his loving presence... The Eucharist is the ladder, not of Jacob, but of Jesus, who mounts to heaven and descends continually for us. He is in an unceasing movement towards us.[83]
I will answer as in the days of her youth	He is there, this Heart, to defend us from our enemies, as a mother, in order to save her child from a danger, holds him against her heart so that the child may not be reached without reaching the mother. And, Jesus tells us, even if a mother could forget her child, I will never abandon you.[84]
You will call me "my husband"	Jesus will have two thrones, one of glory in heaven, another of sweetness and goodness on earth; two courts: the celestial and triumphant court and the court of his redeemed ones here below. In what state does Jesus remain with us? In a state of change, from one time to another? No, rather in a state of perseverance. He stays for ever until the end of the world.[85]

Mercy in Hosea	Mercy in the Eucharist
I will remove the names of the Baals from your mouth	"It is not only that Penance leads to the Eucharist, but that the Eucharist also leads to Penance."[86]
I will abolish the bow, the sword, war	Jesus said to Faustina: "Mankind will not find peace so long as it does not turn with confidence to my mercy."[87] "The throne of mercy is the tabernacle."[88]
I will make for you a covenant; I will espouse you for ever in steadfast love and mercy	We like to penetrate a veiled truth, to discover a hidden treasure, to overcome a difficulty. Thus the faithful soul, in the presence of the Eucharistic veil, seeks her Lord, like Magdalen at the tomb: her desire grows, she calls him like the bride of the Canticle, she pleases herself in giving him all beauties, in decorating him with all glories. The Eucharist is for her what God is for the blessed, a truth, a beauty ever ancient, ever new, that one never wearies of contemplating, of penetrating. Only our Lord's wisdom and goodness could invent the Eucharistic veil.[89]

STAGE 21

Parable of the Marriage Feast
Baptism and Confession

"Have you never read in the Scriptures: 'The very stone which the builders rejected has become the cornerstone; this was the Lord's doing, and it is marvellous in our eyes'? Therefore I tell you, the kingdom of God will be taken away from you and given to a nation producing the fruits of it"... And again Jesus spoke to them in parables, saying, "The kingdom of heaven may be compared to a king who gave a marriage feast for his son, and sent his servants to call those who were invited to the marriage feast; but they would not come. Again he sent other servants, saying, 'Tell those who are invited, Behold, I have made ready my dinner, my oxen and my fat calves are killed, and everything is ready; come to the marriage feast.' But they made light of it and went off, one to his farm, another to his business, while the rest seized his servants, treated them shamefully, and killed them. The king was angry, and he sent his troops and destroyed those murderers and burned their city. Then he said to his servants, 'The wedding is ready, but those invited were not worthy. Go therefore to the streets, and invite to the marriage feast as many as you find.' And those servants went out into the streets and gathered all whom they found, both bad and good; so the wedding hall was filled with guests. But when the king came in to look at the guests, he saw there a man who had no wedding garment; and he said to him, 'Friend, how did you get in here without a wedding garment?' And he was speechless. Then the king said to the attendants, 'Bind him hand and foot, and cast him into the outer darkness, where there will be weeping and gnashing of teeth.' For many are called, but few are chosen."

(*Mt* 21:42-43; 22:1-14)

In Matthew 21:42, Jesus cites the passage of Psalm 118 (22-24) about the stone rejected by the builders but chosen by God. What parable immediately follows? Why does the evangelist illustrate the passage of Psalm 118 with the wedding banquet?

Those invited show themselves to be unworthy to participate in the wedding feast of the king's son because they put their priorities elsewhere. In finding excuses for turning down the invitation, those invited show contempt for the man who invited them as well as for the prepared banquet. For us today, what is the wedding meal? In this wedding, who is the bridegroom? Who is the bride? What food do we receive? How do we respond to this invitation?

One of the guests is not wearing the wedding attire. What does this wedding garment represent? By the sacrament of baptism, the baptised is dressed in the wedding garment and receives the dignity of a child of God. While putting on the white garment, the priest says to the newly baptised: "You have become a new creation, and have clothed yourself in Christ. Receive this baptismal garment and bring it unstained to the judgement seat of our Lord Jesus Christ so that you may have everlasting life." The soul of the baptised becomes the bride, chosen by Christ, who is the spouse. The wedding is inaugurated by baptism. The wedding is consummated by the Eucharist. Thus baptism and Eucharist seal the covenant between the soul and Jesus for eternal life.

He who has not put on the garment at the feast is excluded from it: "Bind him hand and foot, and cast him into the outer darkness." By baptism, we are uprooted from original sin and freed from the power of the demon. The priest makes this prayer of exorcism: "Almighty God…your Son died and rose again to save us. By his victory over sin and death, bring this child out of the power of darkness." Later, the baptised receives the light of Christ with this warning: "Receive the light of Christ… This child…has been enlightened by Christ. He is to walk always as a child of light."

Nevertheless the new life received at baptism "has not abolished the frailty and weakness of human nature, nor the inclination to sin that tradition calls *concupiscence*" (*CCC* 1426).

St Paul expressed his interior combat between good and evil like thus: "For I do not do the good I want, but the evil I do not want is what I do" (*Rm* 7:19). St John reminds us that we are all sinners: "If we say we have not sinned, we make him a liar, and his word is not in us. My little children, I am writing this to you so that you may not sin; but if any one does sin, we have an advocate with the Father, Jesus Christ the righteous" (*1 Jn* 1:10-2:1). Recognising that man would sin despite his baptism and despite the light of the Word of God, Jesus instituted in his mercy the sacrament of confession or reconciliation for "all sinful members of his Church: above all for those who, since baptism, have fallen into grave sin, and have thus lost their baptismal grace and wounded ecclesial communion" (*CCC* 1446). The Resurrected One, conqueror of sin and death, said to his apostles, his first priests: "Peace be with you... Receive the Holy Spirit. If you forgive the sins of any, they are forgiven" (*Jn* 20:21-23).

Being excluded from the feast means passing up the grace that the feast is ordered to give. In our Eucharistic interpretation, this is equivalent to not receiving the grace that the sacrament of the Eucharist is ordered to transmit. In other words, if someone communicates in a state of grave sin without first having been purified in the sacrament of reconciliation, the Eucharist will not bear the desired fruit. On the contrary, his Communion will be sterile. "Communicating without being in communion" could only hurt his incorporation into the Church. How miserable this is! This is why the Church asks believers to confess once a year at a minimum, but strongly encourages frequent confession with individual absolution, to enable approaching the sacrament of the Eucharist worthily, following the words of St Paul: "Let a man examine himself, and so eat of the bread and drink of the cup" (*1 Co* 11:28) . In the sacrament of confession, we of course confess our sins by admitting them according to number and kind, but above all we confess the love of God, conqueror of our sins! Divine mercy finds its source in the Eucharist but transmits itself in a unique way through reconciliation. John Paul II shows the intimate link between the sacrament of reconciliation or penance and the Eucharist.

"Let a man examine himself, and so eat of the bread and drink of the cup." This call by the apostle indicates at least indirectly the close link between the Eucharist and Penance. Indeed, if the first word of Christ's teaching, the first phrase of the Gospel Good News, was "Repent, and believe in the gospel" (*metanoeite*), the Sacrament of the Passion, cross and Resurrection seems to strengthen and consolidate in an altogether special way this call in our souls. The Eucharist and Penance thus become in a sense two closely connected dimensions of authentic life in accordance with the spirit of the Gospel, of truly Christian life. The Christ who calls to the Eucharistic banquet is always the same Christ who exhorts us to penance and repeats his "Repent." Without this constant ever renewed endeavour for conversion, partaking of the Eucharist would lack its full redeeming effectiveness and there would be a loss or at least a weakening of the special readiness to offer God the spiritual sacrifice in which our sharing in the priesthood of Christ is expressed in an essential and universal manner. In Christ, priesthood is linked with his Sacrifice, his self-giving to the Father; and, precisely because it is without limit, that self-giving gives rise in us human beings subject to numerous limitations to the need to turn to God in an ever more mature way and with a constant, ever more profound, conversion.[90]

Let us welcome divine mercy as often as possible through the sacrament of reconciliation. This sacrament deploys in the soul not only God's forgiveness but also interior healing and the strength to fight against the soul's imperfections. It helps us to love God and our neighbour better. Above all it reveals to us the true face of the Father, the face of mercy and tenderness.

Many priests who have set up perpetual adoration in their parish testify to a growing demand for the sacrament of reconciliation as a fruit of Eucharistic adoration. The growth is not only in quantity but also in quality. One cannot stay before the Blessed Sacrament without the light of Christ profoundly illuminating the soul and enlightening the conscience.

"Unless the Lord builds the house, those who build it labour in vain. Unless the Lord watches over the city, the watchman stays awake in vain" (*Ps* 127:1).

STAGE 22

Marriage in the Bible

The man gave names to all cattle, and to the birds of the air, and to every beast of the field; but for the man there was not found a helper fit for him. So the Lord God caused a deep sleep to fall upon the man, and while he slept took one of his ribs and closed up its place with flesh; and the rib which the Lord God had taken from the man he made into a woman and brought her to the man. Then the man said, "This at last is bone of my bones and flesh of my flesh; she shall be called Woman, because she was taken out of Man." Therefore a man leaves his father and his mother and clings to his wife, and they become one flesh. (*Gn* 2:20-24)

This passage from the second story of creation recalls the "day that the Lord God made the earth and the heavens" (*Gn* 2:4). The two stories of creation (*Gn* 1 and 2) are complementary; each sheds a unique light on man, on what he must do, where he comes from, and where he is going. Genesis does not claim to give a scientific explanation of the origin of the world; rather, it speaks to us about man, God, his love, and the work of God so that man might live with him for ever. With regard to the biblical texts that precede Abraham, we should avoid two extreme positions:

that which claims that all that is contained in the biblical texts must be read as modern scientific descriptions and that which, on the contrary, claims that these texts are but a series of tales or legends devoid of historical ties. No, the first chapters of Genesis do not evoke historical facts, even though they are told with ancient images in a Semitic language more than three thousand years old. The sacred authors were looking, not for scientific truth, but for the profound truth about man and God.

At issue here is marriage between the first man and the first woman. The book of Genesis reminds us that this natural marriage is not a human invention. It is the first covenant sealed by God. The two are now one! God wanted this to be so and not otherwise. Behind this first marriage, another covenant emerges throughout revelation: that between God, who is the Bridegroom, and mankind, who is the bride. All the vocabulary of the Bible is nuptial. Scripture describes a series of covenants (cf. *Stage 16*) that lead up to the great Covenant, new and eternal, that is fulfilled in Jesus Christ. The Old Testament (Covenant) gives way to the New Testament (New Covenant).

The Covenant between God and mankind is eternally sealed when Jesus gives his body to his Bride. On the cross, he, the Bridegroom, hands over his body to the Church, the chosen Bride. Just as Eve is taken from the side of Adam, so too, on the cross, *the Church is born from the open side of Christ*, from which flows water and blood. About the pierced side of Christ, St Ambrose said: "It is now that the Church is founded, now that she is formed, now that she appears, now that she is created."[91] Likewise, Adam's mysterious sleep prefigures Christ's death on the cross before his glorious Resurrection. Through his Incarnation, Jesus is united to all mankind. Through his suffering, Jesus saves men: he makes of them children of God. We become his people, acquired at great price: "taking...his own blood, thus securing an eternal redemption" (*Heb* 9:12, cf. *1 P* 2:9).

The sacrament of marriage possesses the particularity among the other sacraments of sanctifying a natural reality that existed before the coming of Christ. In the natural love of man and woman God put an image of his faithful love for men. Even though sin has come and darkened the consciousness of what a true love implies, the spouses are naturally called to a reciprocal and indissoluble gift of their person. This reality of natural marriage has received a new dimension through the coming of Christ, who not only restored the initial order of creation but, in handing himself over, has loved the Church as her only Bridegroom. So that Christian marriage is truly the sign of the New Covenant between God and men, and it can only be this sign if it does not lie about the reality that it designates: the union between Christ and the Church is indissoluble. This is the foundation of the sacrament of marriage and what Christian spouses bear witness to for the world. "What therefore God has joined together, let no man put asunder" (*Mt* 19:6): in taking this commandment of Christ seriously, the Church reaffirms its mystery and calls Christians to live from it in the sacrament that makes it manifest, sure that God has provided in it an irreplaceable means of sanctification.[92]

Pharisees came up and in order to test him asked, "Is it lawful for a man to divorce his wife?" He answered them, "What did Moses command you?" They said, "Moses allowed a man to write a certificate of divorce, and to put her away." But Jesus said to them, "For your hardness of heart he wrote you this commandment. But from the beginning of creation, 'God made them male and female.' 'For this reason a man shall leave his father and mother and be joined to his wife, and the two shall become one flesh.' So they are no longer two but one flesh. What therefore God has joined together, let not man put asunder." (*Mk* 10:2-9)

Jesus is asked to clarify himself on the thorny question of the indissolubility of marriage. First Jesus recalls a prescription of Moses authorising divorce under certain conditions. But he recalls that at the time of Moses, man did not have access to the fullness of grace and truth. "For the law was given through Moses; grace and truth came through Jesus Christ" (*Jn* 1:17). This allowed for a tolerance about divorce. From now on, the presence of Jesus in the heart of his Church is the source of all grace. He promises to give the necessary help to those who ask it of him. It is by prayer and conversion that we obtain the graces to stay fast in love, to learn to forgive, to achieve sanctity in doing the will of God to the very end.

Jesus thus recalls that marriage, according to the plan of God, is indissoluble: "What therefore God has joined together, let not man put asunder." Some ask why the Church does not want to bless a new union between two people who are seeking to rebuild their lives after the failure of their marriages. One might ask oneself why priests do not show more compassion or mercy, since Jesus forgave all sins and since the priest is there to give divine mercy freely. These biblical texts show that Jesus speaks of marriage in another register. Christ united himself to humanity in an indissoluble way in an eternal marriage by dying on the cross. Sacramental marriage is sealed in the absolutely indissoluble covenant of Christ with his Church. St Paul writes: "Neither death, nor life…nor things present, nor things to come…nor anything else in all creation, will be able to separate us from the love of God in Christ Jesus our Lord" (*Rm* 8:38-39).

To conclude, let us listen to St Paul speaking to us about the Church, Body of Christ, and marriage:

Be subject to one another out of reverence for Christ. Wives, be subject to your husbands, as to the Lord.

For the husband is the head of the wife as Christ is the head of the Church, his body, and is himself its Saviour. As the Church is subject to Christ, so let wives also be subject in everything to their husbands. Husbands, love your wives, as Christ loved the Church and gave himself up for her, that he might sanctify her, having cleansed her by the washing of water with the word, that he might present the Church to himself in splendour, without spot or wrinkle or any such thing, that she might be holy and without blemish. Even so husbands should love their wives as their own bodies. He who loves his wife loves himself. For no man ever hates his own flesh, but nourishes and cherishes it, as Christ does the Church, because we are members of his body. "For this reason a man shall leave his father and mother and be joined to his wife, and the two shall become one flesh." This is a great mystery, and I mean in reference to Christ and the Church. (*Ep* 5:21-32)

The submission of which St Paul speaks in the text is not a kind of servility or abasement of one partner in relation to the other. It recalls the spirit of charity and service that must animate every Christian. Find what St Paul asks of the woman, then of the man. The mutual requirements are of the order of total gift. Find the link between the sacrament of marriage and the marriage of Christ with his Church.

STAGE 23

The Eucharist Makes the Church
Incorporation into the Church
Pharaoh's Dream Interpreted by Joseph

Then Pharaoh said to Joseph, "Behold, in my dream I was standing on the banks of the Nile;... I also saw in my dream seven ears growing on one stalk, full and good; and seven ears, withered, thin, and blighted by the east wind, sprouted after them, and the thin ears swallowed up the seven good ears."...Joseph said to Pharaoh... "God has revealed to Pharaoh what he is about to do... The seven good ears are seven years [of plenty]...the seven empty ears blighted by the east wind are also seven years of famine [which will follow]... Let Pharaoh proceed to appoint overseers over the land, and take the fifth part of the produce of the land of Egypt during the seven plenteous years. And let them gather all the food of these good years that are coming, and lay up grain... for food in the cities, and let them keep it. That food shall be a reserve for the land against the seven years of famine which are to befall the land of Egypt, so that the land may not perish through the famine." (*Gn* 41:17-36)

In this text we can see a prefiguration of the Eucharistic Sacrifice: the seven years of plenty in Egypt can be compared to the abundance of graces obtained by Jesus during his work of redemption. On the cross, Christ obtained all the graces necessary for the salvation of all men, without exception, of all places and all times. This is prefigured by the Egyptian storehouses that contain the wheat necessary for the survival of Egypt and the neighbouring nations for the years of famine. During the years of famine, the nations came to Egypt to buy their food. Likewise, in coming to Mass today, we go and draw from the abundance of graces obtained by Jesus on the cross. In instituting the sacrament of the Eucharist, Jesus anticipates and integrates the sacrifice of the cross and the victory of the Resurrection. Thus, the Eucharist celebrated (the Mass) and contemplated (adoration within and outside of Mass) transmits all the graces necessary for our sanctification and the salvation of the world. The Eucharist celebrated and adored makes us *contemporaries* of the work of redemption. Through the Mass, we draw from the living fonts of salvation, as the Second Vatican Council affirms: "The Most Blessed Eucharist contains the entire spiritual [bounty] of the Church, that is, Christ himself, our Pasch and Living Bread, whose flesh, which lives and creates life through the Holy Spirit, gives life to men."[93]

The foundation and wellspring [of the Church] is the whole *Triduum paschale*, but this is as it were gathered up, foreshadowed and "concentrated" for ever in the gift of the Eucharist. In this gift, Jesus Christ entrusted to his Church the perennial making present of the paschal mystery. With it he brought about a mysterious "oneness in time" between that *Triduum* and the passage of the centuries.[94]

Here now are a few reminders about the nature of the Church, the universal sacrament of salvation, and about our incorporation into her through faith and the seven sacraments.

The Lord Jesus, the only Saviour, did not only establish a simple community of disciples, but constituted the Church as a *salvific mystery*: he himself is in the Church and the Church is in him… Therefore the fullness of Christ's salvific mystery belongs also to the Church, inseparably united to her Lord. Indeed, Jesus Christ continues his presence and his work of salvation in the Church and by means of the Church…, which is his body… And thus, just as the head and the members of a living body, though not identical, are inseparable, so too Christ and the Church can neither be confused nor separated, and constitute a single "whole Christ".[95]

What is the "whole Christ"? The Church is the Body of Christ. Christ is the Head of it, we his members. Through faith in Jesus Christ, the divine life circulates from the Head to the members of the Body. This divine life flows from the redemption.

Above all else, it must be *firmly believed* that "the Church, a pilgrim now on earth, is necessary for salvation: the one Christ is the mediator and the way of salvation; he is present to us in his body which is the Church. He himself explicitly asserted the necessity of faith and baptism (cf. *Mk* 16:16; *Jn* 3:5), and thereby affirmed at the same time the necessity of the Church which men enter through baptism as through a door."[96]

In this passage, what are the ties between the Church and salvation? What are the two conditions for being incorporated into the Church, the Body of Christ?

The Church is "the universal sacrament of salvation", since, united always in a mysterious way to the Saviour Jesus Christ, her Head, and subordinated to him, she has, in God's plan, an indispensable relationship with the salvation of every human being. For those who are not formally and visibly members of the Church, salvation in Christ is accessible by virtue of a grace which, while having a mysterious relationship to the Church, does not make them formally part of the Church, but enlightens them in a way which is accommodated to their spiritual and material situation. This grace comes from Christ; it is the fruit of his sacrifice and is communicated by the Holy Spirit; it has a relationship with the Church.[97]

It is in the Mass, then, celebrated on all the altars of the world, that the grace of redemption is made present. This grace is poured out first upon those who participate in the Eucharist, but also, more broadly, upon all men of goodwill.

> With respect to the *way* in which the salvific grace of God – which is always given by means of Christ in the Spirit and has a mysterious relationship to the Church – comes to individual non-Christians, the Second Vatican Council limited itself to the statement that God bestows it "in ways known to himself".[98]

"The bread which I shall give for the life of the world is my flesh" (*Jn* 6:51). The Eucharist is the spiritual sun of the world. As the sun gives life to nature through its heat and light, the Eucharist gives divine life to our souls and its spiritual light to our world. "The world could live without the sun, but not without the Holy Mass" (St Padre Pio).

"*The Church draws her life from Christ in the Eucharist*; by him she is fed and by him she is enlightened."[99] The incorporation into the Church sealed at baptism is extended by virtue of the following sacraments: confirmation, sacramental confession, matrimony, anointing of the sick, Holy Orders. But above all, by sacramental Communion. Let us recall the three distinct dimensions of the Eucharist: the Holy Sacrifice of the Mass, Holy Communion, and adoration outside of Mass (cf. *Stage 1*). Through sacramental Communion, the Lord weds the soul that he comes to visit in giving himself to her: "Blessed are those who are invited to the marriage supper of the Lamb" (*Rv* 19:9). "Take, eat;

this is my body" (*Mt* 26:26); "He who eats my flesh and drinks my blood abides in me, and I in him" (*Jn* 6:56).

> Communion is the complete development, the blooming of the Incarnation. The Body of Jesus Christ thus unites itself to our body, his soul to our soul, and his divinity hovers over both. Our body is, as it were, inserted within the Body of our Lord... Our body takes strength, grace, integrity, morals from his. Let us then leave our body to be reformed in this divine mould and germinate in him for glory. But the soul? Jesus Christ goes directly to our soul. He says to her: "I want to wed you for ever." Above all, the soul is the object Jesus is aiming for in us. The body is but an antechamber: it is the first to be honoured, yet our Lord only passes through it. The soul receives Jesus and transmits his divine life: she is as though lost within our Lord.[100]

The two following passages clarify the extent to which sacramental Communion strengthens incorporation into Christ, which begins with baptism and faith. What are the fruits of sacramental Communion evoked by Pope St John Paul II?

> Incorporation into Christ, which is brought about by baptism, is constantly renewed and consolidated by sharing in the Eucharistic Sacrifice, especially by that full sharing which takes place in sacramental communion. We can say not only that *each of us receives*

Christ, but also that *Christ receives each of us*. He enters into friendship with us: "You are my friends" (*Jn* 15:14). Indeed, it is because of him that we have life: "He who eats me will live because of me" (*Jn* 6:57). Eucharistic communion brings about in a sublime way the mutual abiding of Christ and each of his followers: "Abide in me, and I in you" (*Jn* 15:4).[101]

The saving efficacy of the sacrifice is fully realised when the Lord's body and blood are received in communion. The Eucharistic Sacrifice is intrinsically directed to the inward union of the faithful with Christ through communion; we receive the very One who offered himself for us, we receive his body which he gave up for us on the cross and his blood which he "poured out for many for the forgiveness of sins" (*Mt* 26:28). We are reminded of his words: "As the living Father sent me, and I live because of the Father, so he who eats me will live because of me" (*Mt* 6:57).[102]

Let us now consider the difficult question of the relation of those divorced and remarried to the Eucharist.

Divorced and remarried persons "find themselves in a situation that objectively contravenes God's law."[103] "What therefore God has joined together, let not man put asunder" (*Mk* 10:9). The Church does not judge consciences and does not condemn persons. She knows how painful their personal story often is. Nevertheless, divorced and remarried persons cannot be admitted to Eucharistic

Communion because "their state and condition of life objectively contradict that union of love between Christ and the Church which is signified and effected by the Eucharist."[104] These persons can feel a real suffering, all the stronger given their great desire to receive the Lord. Those who abstain from receiving Communion through fidelity to the Church do not distance themselves from Christ. On the contrary, they come closer to him.

Even though they cannot, for the time being, receive Eucharistic Communion, as baptised persons, they remain members of the Church.

The imprint of baptism is not erased. They are thus invited to participate in the life of the Church: "to listen to the word of God, to attend the Sacrifice of the Mass, to persevere in prayer, to contribute to works of charity".[105] Thus, they are called to draw abundantly from the graces that flow from the Eucharist, not by sacramental Communion, but by spiritual communion during Mass and also in adoration of the Blessed Sacrament.

Despite a suffering that will always remain sharp, by their persevering faith that pushes them to come to Mass all the same, and by their witness of obedience to the Church who asks them to abstain from Communion, they remind others of the grace they are granted in being able to unite themselves to Christ through sacramental Communion and of how much this is a gift and never something owed them.

"With firm confidence, [the Church] believes that even those who have rejected the Lord's command and are still living in this state will be able to obtain from God the grace of conversion and salvation, provided that they have persevered in prayer, penance and charity."[106]

Contemplation prolongs Communion and enables one to encounter Christ, true God and true man, in a lasting way, to let oneself be looked upon by him, and to experience his presence. When we contemplate him present in the Blessed Sacrament of the altar, Christ draws near and more intimate to us than we are to ourselves: he gives us a part of his divine life in a transforming union and, through the Spirit, he gives us access to the Father, as he himself said to Philip: "He who has seen me has seen the Father" (*Jn* 14:9). Contemplation, which is also a communion of desire, intimately associates us with Christ and, in a very special way, associates those who are prevented from receiving him.[107]

Salvation comes from God alone; but because we receive the life of faith through the Church, she is our mother: "We believe the Church as the mother of our new birth, and not *in* the Church as if she were the author of our salvation." Because she is our mother, she is also our teacher in the faith.[108]

The marriage that Jesus Christ desires to enter into with our soul...through the most adorable Eucharist...

Where is the banquet of this royal wedding held? It is in the bosom of your soul, which is a magnificent palace that the heavenly King has had adorned with his wonderful riches, which are his divine virtues, his gifts, and his mercies. There in surplus are all the graces and merits of Jesus the Bridegroom that he gives as a gift to your soul. The witnesses to this holy marriage are the Divine Persons of the Father and the Holy Spirit, and the eternal Word pronounces these mysterious words found in Holy Scripture, speaking to your soul: "I marry you in faith." This is so profound and so true that this holy marriage is renewed each time you receive Communion… Prefer nothing to the love of Jesus Christ, but be careful not to come without your wedding gown, which shows the purity of the heart… or the purity of our intentions. Let us do all things according to the divine will. This intent keeps our soul apart from all that is not God and arrays it in the holy dispositions of Jesus Christ. And for the time being she is dressed in the wedding gown and able to be admitted to the magnificent and sublime banquet in which she is satisfied by God himself with such abundance that the soul that has once eaten him as she should, with the necessary dispositions, will never again hunger for the things of the earth. Oh! How well does the soul that in faith eats Jesus Christ in the sacred Host understand what I am saying! All creatures become tasteless to her, and she can only delight in the one taste of Jesus her Bridegroom, which she finds better than wine.[109]

Eucharistic Communion strengthens the unity of the Church, the Body of Christ. "The bread which we break, is it not a participation in the body of Christ? Because there is one bread, we who are many are one body, for we all partake of the one bread" (*1 Co* 10:16-17). St John Chrysostom is more specific:

> "For what is this bread? It is the Body of Christ. And what do those who receive it become? The Body of Christ – not many bodies but one body. For as bread is completely one, though made up of many grains of wheat, and these albeit unseen, remain nonetheless present, in such a way that their difference is not apparent since they have been made a perfect whole, so too are we mutually joined to one another and together united with Christ."[110] "The seeds of disunity, which daily experience shows to be so deeply rooted in humanity as a result of sin, are countered by *the unifying power* of the body of Christ. The Eucharist, precisely by building up the Church, creates human community."[111]

STAGE 24

The Suffering Servant and Kenosis

He had no form or comeliness that we should look at him, and no beauty that we should desire him. He was despised and rejected by men; a man of sorrows, and acquainted with grief; and as one from whom men hide their faces he was despised, and we esteemed him not. Surely he has borne our griefs and carried our sorrows; yet we esteemed him stricken, struck down by God, and afflicted. But he was wounded for our transgressions, he was bruised for our iniquities; upon him was the chastisement that made us whole, and with his stripes we are healed. All we like sheep have gone astray; we have turned everyone to his own way; and the Lord has laid on him the iniquity of us all. He was oppressed, and he was afflicted, yet he opened not his mouth; like a lamb that is led to the slaughter, and like a sheep that before its shearers is silent, so he opened not his mouth. By oppression and judgement he was taken away; and as for his generation, who considered that he was cut off out of the land of the living, stricken for the transgression of my people? And they made his grave with the wicked and with a rich man in his death, although he had done no violence, and there was no deceit in his mouth. Yet it was the will of the Lord to bruise him; he has put him to grief; when he makes himself an offering for sin, he shall see his offspring, he shall prolong his days; the will of the Lord shall prosper in his hand; he shall see the fruit of the travail of his soul and be satisfied; by his knowledge shall the righteous one, my servant, make many to be accounted righteous; and he shall bear their iniquities. Therefore I will divide him a portion with the great, and he shall divide the spoil with the strong; because he poured out his soul to death, and was numbered with the transgressors; yet he bore the sin of many, and made intercession for the transgressors. (*Is* 53:2-12)

The table on pages 160-161 shows the parallels between the prophecy of the suffering servant (*Is* 53), the bloody Passion of Jesus on his bloody way to Golgotha (*Jn* 11, *Jn* 19 and *Jn* 20), and the permanent presence of Jesus the Host on his mystical Calvary in the tabernacles of the world. These parallels only take up the first part of Isaiah 53. Others can be established by glancing through the end of Isaiah 53.

By kenosis, God empties himself of his glory in order to meet fallen man:

Though he was in the form of God, [he] did not count equality with God a thing to be grasped, but emptied himself, taking the form of a servant, being born in the likeness of men. And being found in human form he humbled himself and became obedient unto death, even death on a cross. Therefore God has highly exalted him and bestowed on him the name which is above every name, that at the name of Jesus every knee should bow, in heaven and on earth and under the earth, and every tongue confess that Jesus Christ is Lord, to the glory of God the Father. (*Ph* 2:6-11)

That the Son of God so loved the world that he made himself man, we understand: the Creator must have it in his heart to repair the work of his hands. That the Man-God died on the cross, we still understand through an excess of love. But what stops being understandable, what amazes those weak in faith and scandalises unbelievers, is that Jesus Christ, glorious, crowned, having achieved his mission here below, still desires to remain with us, and in a state more humbled, more dejected than at Bethlehem, or even than at Calvary. Let us raise with respect the mysterious veil that covers the Holy of Holies and try to understand the excess of love that the Lord shows for us.[112]

On the cross Christ lowered himself in the extreme in order to show us his love. All the same, in the Blessed Sacrament, he lowers himself even more. There, we no longer even see the Divine Person, but only the appearances of bread. We no longer hear his voice that rang from the cross: "I thirst." In coming to the Blessed Sacrament, he leaves his glory and majesty in heaven and takes the risk of being ignored and forgotten under insignificant appearances. He comes but with his love and his mercy. He seeks souls who will love him for himself. But love is not loved. St Thérèse of Lisieux said: "The nature of love is to humble oneself… Yes, in order that Love be fully satisfied, it is necessary that it lower itself, and that it lower itself to nothingness and transform this nothingness into *fire*."[113]

The following witness helps in understanding why God pushes his Son to such an annihilation: a young woman who had spent a number of years in the street, after having been abandoned by her family, abused by men, and broken by the trials of life, tells how her encounter with Jesus during a period of Eucharistic adoration transformed her life: "I had descended so low, like someone fallen from a precipice into the depths. Darkness surrounded me on all sides. But, at the greatest depth of the abyss, I crashed into Jesus, who took me in his arms and raised me up again towards God my Father. Thank you Jesus!"

Here is how kenosis unfurls in the Eucharist, the memorial of Jesus's Passion:

1. Christ hands himself over in a freely accepted offering. The Eucharist is instituted on *Holy Thursday*, "This is my body given for you, this is my blood poured out for you!" In sovereign freedom, Jesus gives himself.

2. The love freely offered is handed over in the Passion. Jesus undergoes the torments that are inflicted upon him.

He freely carries his cross, lowers his head, and gives up his Spirit. Love consents to be handed over: "No one takes [my life] from me, but I lay it down of my own accord" (*Jn* 10:18). It is a silent sheep that hands itself over! It is the passivity of the Passion: he allows himself to be led! It is a life given up to the last drop of blood. This is *Good Friday*.

3. The offering is accomplished to the end; it is the ultimate abasement of the One who is handed over, in total passivity, to death. It is this state of the Son dead among the dead. He descended to hell in the hell of death. This is the silence of *Holy Saturday*. Jesus is in the tomb.

4. Christ is resurrected *Easter Sunday*. He remains present in his Church until the end of time to pass on his victory over death and the glory of his Resurrection. After the Consecration, the Real Presence of Jesus remains in the Eucharist. "The tabernacle is there to show the definitive state of the Son's offering to the Father and gift to the world. We are pathetically passive. Jesus is present and supremely active. The Prince of Life is intensely active, and it is up to us to attune ourselves to Jesus's transfiguring and deeply moving presence."[114] But to the Real Presence of Jesus we often respond with our real absence!

Jesus will have two thrones, one of glory in heaven, another of sweetness and goodness on earth; two courts: the celestial and triumphant court and the court of his redeemed ones here below. In what state does Jesus remain with us? In a state of change, from one time to another? No, rather, in a state of perseverance. He stays for ever until the end of the world.

But, O marvel of the Eucharist! Through his sacramental state, Jesus gives new homage to his Father such as the Father has never received from any creature; a greater homage, so to say, than all that the Word incarnate could do on earth. What, then, is this extraordinary homage? It is the homage of the King of glory, consummated in power and the majesty of heaven, who comes in his sacrament to immolate to his Father, not only his divine glory as in the Incarnation, but even his human glory, the glorious qualities of his resurrected humanity![115]

Song of the Suffering Servant (*Is* 53)	Jesus during his Passion (*Jn* 19)	Jesus present in the Eucharist, memorial of the Passion
"no form or comeliness that we should look at him"	"Here is the man" (*Jn* 19:5)	the still Host
"no beauty that we should desire him"	"Crucify him" (*Jn* 19:6)	Jesus truly present, under the appearances of bread
"despised"	"Hail, King of the Jews" (*Jn* 19:3)	too often considered as a thing, or at best a simple food

"rejected by men"	abandoned by those he healed, fed, taught	abandoned in the tabernacles of the world
"A man of sorrows, and acquainted with grief; and as one from whom men hide their faces he was despised, and we esteemed him not"	betrayed by Judas; denied by Peter; a criminal is preferred to the sweet Saviour who says: "I thirst" (Jn 19:28)	What does he do in the Blessed Sacrament? "He awaits us" (Curé of Ars). "My thirst to be loved in the Blessed Sacrament is so great that it consumes me" (Jesus to St Margaret Mary).
"Surely he has borne our griefs and carried our sorrows"	"He went out, bearing his own cross" (Jn 19:17)	Eucharist is the Lamb of God, who bears the sin of the world, my sin
"He was wounded for our transgressions, he was bruised for our iniquities"	"One of the soldiers pierced his side with a spear, and at once there came out blood and water" (Jn 19:34)	Eucharist flows from the pierced Heart of Jesus; he gives love for hate
"Upon him was the chastisement that made us whole, and with his stripes we are healed"	He shows his glorious wounds (Jn 20:27)	He gives his resurrected Body in the Eucharist that heals us
"All we like sheep have gone astray; we have turned every one to his own way"	"Jesus should die… to gather into one the children of God who are scattered abroad" (Jn 11:51-52)	He is our Shepherd in the Eucharist; his people are the Church; "the Eucharist makes the Church."

STAGE 25

"I Am the Living Bread"

For this stage, use your New Testament at chapter 6 of St John's Gospel.

Part 1: vv. 1-15, The multiplication of the loaves: Jesus shows his desire to feed mankind. He does not accomplish the miracle out of nothing; rather, he uses a child's five loaves and two fishes. This offering, insignificant to the apostles, the Lord welcomes favourably. He multiplies it to feed the large crowd. Likewise, in the offertory during Mass, we give a part of our material goods to the collection. Nevertheless, it is first of all our person and our heart that we offer to the Lord. This offering is brought to the altar in the form of bread and wine. Jesus, in the person of the priest, changes it into his Body and Blood to feed the faithful who are present. Likewise, in adoration, the Lord welcomes the offering of our time and our person, which he uses to bless and spiritually feed so many people who receive a new effect of divine grace: "Through adoration, the Christian contributes to the radical transformation of the world. Every person who prays to the Lord brings the whole world with him, raising the world to God."[116]

For having received bread from him, the crowd wants to make Jesus their king (*Jn* 6:15). But he did not come for a social kingship that consists in giving bread to all. "My kingship is not of this world" (*Jn* 18:36). His kingship is first of all spiritual. In fact, the episode of the multiplication of the loaves prepares the crowds to welcome another food, which does not satisfy the body but gives life to the soul: it is the Eucharist, God's gift for the life of the world. Through the Eucharist, Jesus comes to reign in hearts. His kingdom, although spiritual, must nevertheless have social repercussions, particularly in civil laws, and become concrete through gestures of charity. This episode can be considered the first Eucharistic miracle in the history of the Church.

Part 2: vv. 16-21, Jesus walks on water: While Providence moves first and normally through the natural laws that God has fixed, God is not limited by his laws and can, in his sovereign freedom, act in a supernatural way. In walking on water, Jesus prepares his disciples for his Eucharistic discourse, whose content surpasses the scope of natural laws. In the Eucharist, Jesus gives himself under the sacramental mode, a mode unique in its type and having no equivalent in nature.

Part 3: vv. 22-71, The Eucharistic discourse at Capernaum: In verse 26, the crowds do not grasp that the multiplication of the loaves and Jesus's walking on water were but precursory signs of the discourse on the bread of life. The disciples do not manage to see farther than the earthly food that has satisfied their bodies. They make of the sign an end in itself.

It can happen that we, too, through a lack of faith, see in the Eucharist only the sign or the appearances of bread, without discerning the real, bodily, substantial presence of Jesus.

In verse 27, Jesus invites his disciples to seek first the "food which endures to eternal life". This is why the Church has always desired that Sunday be a public holiday, so that every Christian might have the time to go and receive the true food at Mass, given by God himself, more essential for man than the "food which perishes" (*Jn* 6:27).

"This is the work of God, that you *believe* in him whom he has sent" (*Jn* 6:29). In the context of the Eucharistic discourse, it is not only about *believing* in Jesus seated at the right hand of the Father, but also about *believing* precisely in Jesus who gives himself in the Eucharist. This is what God desires for us and what he accomplishes by his grace.

In rereading verses 29, 32, 38, 44 and 45, note the verbs used by Jesus to speak of the Father's action towards him. The work of the Father is to render all glory to the Son – this glory that the Son gives to him in perfectly doing his will. It is the Father who gives this food. He gives faith for believing in this presence. He leads towards Jesus, draws us to him, and glorifies him.

Remember that before the Son became incarnate and gave himself in the Eucharist on earth:

He was from all eternity in a position of (Eucharistic) "availability" to the Father, an attitude of offering so absolute that in the eyes of the Father it appeared as the prefiguration of the cross. St Peter expresses this in his first epistle: Christ was known beforehand by the Father as the Lamb giving his blood for us, even before the creation of the world (*1 P* 1:20), thus, precisely when he put himself at the disposal of the Father for us; when he, as it were, "interposed" himself so that the arrows of sin that the world sends to God reach, not the Father, but himself (Adrienne von Speyr).[117]

In verses 32-34, Jesus explains that the manna received from God during the Exodus prefigured the Eucharist. Jesus is himself the new manna that gives what the old manna could not: eternal life.

Preliminary reflections on faith: Faith is first of all a grace, a gift of God: when Peter confesses that Jesus is the Christ, the Son of the living God, Jesus declares to him that this revelation has come to him, not from "flesh and blood..., but [from] my Father who is in heaven" (*Mt* 16:17). Faith is a gift of God, a supernatural virtue infused by him.

To make this act of faith, the grace of God and the interior help of the Holy Spirit must precede and assist, moving the heart and turning it to God, opening the eyes of the mind and giving "joy and ease to everyone in assenting to the truth and believing it."[118]

Faith is also the adequate response of man to the Father's invitation: by his revelation, "the invisible God...speaks to men as friends and lives among them, so that he may invite and take them into fellowship with himself."[119]

Just after the Consecration, the priest proclaims: "The mystery of faith". The Church's faith finds its culmination in the Eucharist. The Eucharist recapitulates, concentrates, and makes present anew all the mysteries of the life of Christ. In welcoming faith in the Eucharist, we believe that the Son became incarnate in Jesus, died for our sins, was resurrected to give us eternal life, and leads us through his Spirit. We believe that the Holy Sacrifice of the Mass, celebrated in the Church, makes redemption present. We believe that Jesus gives himself in food to fortify the divine life received at baptism. We believe that he remains among us in the tabernacle as our travel companion and that he pushes us to love one another: "Greater love has no man than this, that a man lay down his life for his friends" (*Jn* 15:13). He asks us to become witnesses of his love that gives itself to the end in the Eucharist. For the fullness of the divine life is transmitted by his Body, which is the Church and whose heart is the Eucharist: "For in him the whole fullness of deity dwells bodily" (*Col* 2:9).

The holy Eucharist is truly the Sacrament of faith. The Eucharist roots our faith ever more in the Passion of Christ and in his pierced Heart. This is the source of the authentic faith that gives us this assurance: "Faith is the assurance of things hoped for, the conviction of things not seen" (*Heb* 11:1). And when doubt seems to carry it away, let us approach nearer to the Eucharist, at Mass and in adoration. Faith, while radiant, is often lived in darkness, because "we walk by faith, not by sight" (*2 Co* 5:7). Faith is never tangible, but the Eucharist fortifies it in such a way that it makes us able to move mountains!

Vv. 35-47: Spiritual communion and adoration: For the Eucharist to strengthen the divine life in the soul, faith in the Real Presence is indispensable. The greater the intensity of a man's faith, the preparation of his heart, and his desire to receive Jesus, the more does the Eucharist nourish his heart. Be sure to note that in this passage the question is not yet of receiving sacramental Communion. Rather the elements of spiritual communion are brought together. These are three verbs that Jesus uses for spiritually communicating with his Eucharistic Body: come, see, and believe.

"For this is the will of my Father, that everyone who sees the Son and believes in him should have eternal life" (*Jn* 6:40). This verse is made clear by the passage about the bronze serpent in Numbers 21:4-9. The Israelites, who had sinned, were bitten by serpents. In order not to die, they had to direct their gaze toward a sign: "And as Moses lifted up the serpent in the wilderness, so must the Son of man be lifted up, that whoever believes in him may have eternal life" (*Jn* 3:14). In what way can Jesus compare himself to a serpent when he was suspended from the wood of the cross? John 3:14 recalls that the salvation offered by Jesus comes from the cross. John 6:40, the heart of the Eucharistic discourse, shows that the salvation offered on the cross is realised in the soul by approaching the Eucharist with faith. Through the Eucharist, Jesus desires to save every man, without exception, for "this is the will of him who sent me, that I should lose nothing of all that he has given me" (*Jn* 6:39). Thus the salvation of mankind is received through the Eucharist, which makes present for us the victory of Jesus on the cross, a victory prefigured by the bronze serpent in the desert. The Eucharist is truly the memorial of the Passion.

STAGE 26

"I Am the Living Bread" (*continued*)

For this stage, use your New Testament at chapter 6 of St John's Gospel.

Vv. 51-58, Sacramental Communion (banquet): In these verses, the verb used is "to eat". In Greek, the verb *trôgô* is translated literally as "to chew", "to masticate". Thus, after having discerned through faith the Body of Christ in the Eucharist and after having contemplated and adored it, it is necessary to "eat" this food. It nourishes and fortifies the baptismal life, also called eternal life, supernatural life, or divine life. The Eucharist is the ordinary food that God gives to his children to fortify his divine life in them. The sacramental mode is unique in creation. God uses this mode to strengthen the indwelling of the Divine Persons in the soul of the just man. Through sacramental Communion, the indwelling of the Divine Persons becomes more interior, more intimate.

St Augustine puts these words in the mouth of Jesus: I am the food of grown men: grow and you shall feed on me; you shall not change me like the food of your flesh into what you are but you shall be changed into what I am.[120] "It is no longer I who live, but Christ who lives in me" (*Ga* 2:20). Through Eucharistic Communion, we remain in Jesus (cf.

Jn 6:56). This life is not in us like water in a container, rather it is we who are like a sponge in an ocean of divine life.

Following Leviticus 9:4, it was forbidden to drink the blood of an animal. All the more reason why drinking the blood of a man (cf. *Jn* 6:53) provokes a scandal with the Jews. In fact, Jesus announces the New Covenant, sealed by his Blood spilled on the cross and made present in each Eucharist. This covenant, while prefigured by the former covenants, brings with it a radically new dimension: it is necessary to drink the Blood of Christ. The blood, in the Semitic language, is the seat of life. It is the soul. When Jesus gives his Body, he gives himself in person, with all he is and all he has. In giving his Blood separately from the Body, he gives, in addition, his death. More precisely, he gives his love that extends to offering his life. He cannot give more than his Body and his Blood. Note Jesus's sacrificial vocabulary: to eat the Body that has been given up and drink from the spilled Blood recalls that the Mass is *first of all a sacrifice and, then, a meal*, like the fruit that a tree bears.

On three occasions (vv. 41, 52, 61), the Jews "murmur", as they did many times during the Exodus. The following verses explain the gravity of murmuring, unveiling this spirit of contestation that attracts divine wrath: "The people became impatient on the way. And the people spoke against God and against Moses, 'Why have you brought us up out of Egypt to die in the wilderness? For there is no food and no water, and we loathe this worthless food'" (*Nb* 21:4-5). God can do nothing more for his people if they are disgusted by the manna, this food that is supposed to enable them to reach the Promised Land. Likewise for us, if we are scandalised or revolted by the Eucharist, what can give us eternal life and enable us to reach the heavenly city?

This same form of contestation about the bread of life stirs up the crowds listening to the Eucharistic discourse. They are scandalised by the "realism" of this food that Jesus announces. There is no other alternative: either Jesus is speaking in a *symbolic or metaphorical* way (for example, we can say: he is as strong as a lion, or he eats like an ogre, without for all that being a lion or an ogre!), or what Jesus is saying must be interpreted *literally*, which is in fact the faith of the Church. Jesus is truly the "bread of life"; we must eat his flesh and drink his blood to grow in divine life. If Jesus was speaking symbolically, the Jews would have accepted his words. No, Jesus prefers to lose his disciples, those he has fed, healed, those who have accompanied him from the beginning of his ministry. Jesus cannot compromise on this truth. So we sadly note the first schism in the Church as yet being born:

"After this many of his disciples drew back and no longer walked with him" (*Jn* 6:66). For the first time, it is his disciples and no longer those opposing him who separate themselves from him. They cannot receive the truth about the Eucharist.

"It is the Spirit that gives life, the flesh is of no avail; the words that I have spoken to you are Spirit and life" (*Jn* 6:63). The words about the Eucharist scandalise them. Jesus reproaches them for listening to the spoken Word in too human and fleshly a way and not spiritually. It is the Spirit that is going to give life to the body of Christ in the tomb and who will resurrect him from the dead. In Communion, we receive sacramentally the body of Jesus dead and resurrected, and not his body in its natural presence. Only the Spirit can give understanding about this food.

"Lord, to whom shall we go? You have the words of eternal life" (*Jn* 6:68). That is the greatness of Peter's faith! He does not understand everything, but he welcomes this truth, for he knows that "with God nothing will be impossible" (*Lk* 1:37). It is this assent of faith that we must imitate. By faith, man submits his intellect and his will to God. With all his being, man gives his assent to the God who reveals himself. No one can understand the Eucharist intellectually or scientifically, because the sacramental mode surpasses natural laws. Nevertheless, Jesus is the Truth; thus, he cannot lie. The Eucharist is the Sacrament of faith par excellence.

During the creation of the world, what the Word commands is immediately achieved. He said "let there be light" and "there was light" (*Gn* 1:3). Likewise, when the Word incarnate, Jesus, said: "This is my body", the intellect understands only that God is capable of it, and, if Jesus works this miracle, it is for our salvation. The intellect can only adore this mystery. Our faith is nourished on it!

We need the Church in order to believe in the Real Presence. Without her, it is not possible to believe in it. For this reason, Peter does not speak in the first person singular but uses the first person plural: "We have believed, and have come to know, that you are the Holy One of God" (*Jn* 6:69). It is the faith of the Church that we receive. It is in the Church that we believe. The Church lives from the Eucharist, and the Eucharist makes the Church.

> Faith is a personal act – the free response of the human person to the initiative of God who reveals himself. But faith is not an isolated act. No one can believe alone, just as no one can live alone. You have not given yourself faith as you have not given yourself life. The believer has received faith from others and should hand it on to others. Our love for Jesus and for our neighbour impels us to speak to others about our faith. Each believer is thus a link in the great chain of believers. I cannot believe without being carried by the faith of others, and by my faith I help support others in the faith.[121]

> Faith is *certain*. It is more certain than all human knowledge because it is founded on the very word of God who cannot lie. To be sure, revealed truths can seem obscure to human reason and experience, but "the certainty that the divine light gives is greater than that which the light of natural reason gives." "Ten thousand difficulties do not make one doubt."[122]

During Communion, we receive neither bread nor a symbol, but the reality itself of the Body of Christ, Jesus himself in person. This divine food is without price! A single Communion has more value than all the world's gold, because through it, Christ resurrected gives himself completely. St John Chrysostom said: "Terrible, truly terrible are the mysteries of the Church, terrible is the altar. Without the special help of the grace of God, no soul could withstand the fire of this food without being entirely destroyed." And he also said that after Communion, "the Christian is like a fearsome lion with flames coming forth from his mouth. The devil cannot withstand the sight of him."

To distinguish and not risk confusing the "bread of life" and the bread that nourishes the body, Benedict XVI invites adoration of this heavenly food. He says, taking up the words of St Augustine:

> "No one should eat this flesh without first adoring it;… we should sin were we not to adore it."… Indeed, we do not merely receive something in the Eucharist. It is the encounter and unification of persons; the person, however, who comes to meet us and desires to unite himself to us is the Son of God. Such unification can only be brought about by means of adoration. Receiving the Eucharist means adoring the One whom we receive.[123]

The Word feeds the soul, but the Word incarnate feeds the body by giving it a seed of immortality.

STAGE 27

Isaac's Blessing and Transubstantiation

St Thomas Aquinas, termed the Doctor of the Eucharist, is part of the line of great witnesses who were truly penetrated by this mystery of the Eucharist. One day while celebrating Mass at Naples, he was so profoundly overwhelmed that he no longer had any desire to write. He suspended the writing of the *Summa Theologiae*. His brother Reginald asked him why he was interrupting such a work. Thomas answered him: "I cannot go on, because all I have written appears to me so much straw! So much straw compared to what has been shown and revealed to me [at the Mass]." And yet, had God not said to him:

"Thomas, you have spoken well of me"?[124]

Thomas had just set out in his *Summa* the nine great wonders of the Eucharist presented below. For these wonders, it is necessary to distinguish clearly the substance of a thing (what exists in itself, the profound being) and the accidents or appearance or species of this thing (what is accessible to our senses and enables us to understand the substance):

1. The first wonder is that under the appearance of bread the true Body of Christ is present, under the species of the humble host is found the Creator of heaven and earth;

2. The substance of the bread is changed into the true Body of Christ. This Body is the same that was formed in the womb of the Virgin Mary, because there is only one Jesus, who really took flesh from the Virgin Mary;

3. Nothing of the bread is left, except for an appearance. But the appearance does not make bread, bread: it is its substance. Yet, the substance of the bread has been entirely changed into the Body of Jesus without altering the appearances of bread – the colour, taste, exterior form;

4. It is not a small bit of Jesus that we find in the Host; the Body of Christ in its entirety is under the appearance of a small host;

5. Another wonder of the Eucharist: one and the same Body is in its entirety in many places, in many Hosts, in many portions;

6. This Body of Jesus in many places, however, remains one. It is not divided or broken into pieces, but remains whole and undivided;

7. When we take the Body of Christ to be nourished from it, it is not at all diminished;

8. If the Body of Christ is not eaten, it is in some way diminished insofar as we are all together one same Body

since we participate in one bread (*1 Co* 10:17). And when Christians able to communicate do not do so, they prevent the construction of the mystical Body of Christ... The Body of Christ in the Host thus builds the Body of Christ that is the Church. It is by communicating and receiving the grace of Communion that the Church is built up and becomes an ever more visible sign of God's Real Presence in the heart of mankind;

9. The Body of Christ is increased when we communicate, because those who communicate are called to convert themselves and will be changed into the Body of Christ. It is thus the holy Church, whose border is located in our hearts, that grows (cf. *Ep* 4:10).[125]

All these wonders concerning the Eucharist, which the Church sums up in the word *transubstantiation*, call for our wonder and demand our assent of faith. The tradition distinguishes the literal and spiritual senses of the great biblical texts.[126] St Thomas Aquinas presents a spiritual interpretation of chapter 27 of Genesis (reread the chapter in your Bible). He sees a type of the discrepancy between faith and the senses in the blessing of Jacob:

> What then has happened? Isaac is ill, agonising, and almost blind. He desires to pass on the blessing to his eldest son, Esau. But his wife, Rebecca, sees things differently and arranges everything so that it is Jacob, the younger son, who receives the blessing and thus his

Father's mission. What at first sight appears a terrible trick is interpreted differently – spiritually – by St Thomas Aquinas. It is not Isaac as such who is deceived, it is his senses: he thought he was blessing Esau when he was touching Jacob, who resembled Esau because of the veil with which he had covered himself.

How then is this applied to the mystery of the Eucharist? In an allegorical interpretation that does not exclude other understandings of the text, Jacob is the type of the Body of the Lord. Isaac and Rebecca, his wife, signify the two natures that are in us: body and soul. The male figure, Isaac, represents the exterior man, the senses. Rebecca, the wife who resides at home and governs the family, represents the soul who cares for its salvation and that of others. Jacob, lovable and good, dwelling in the tent, Rebecca's favourite – that is, the favourite of the faithful soul – signifies the true Body of Jesus. Esau, loved by Isaac, type of the body, signifies the substance of the bread with its accidents: flavour, colour, and its other qualities.

While Isaac – that is, the exterior man – is working the consecration, Esau – or the substance of the bread – is no longer there. But Esau's likeness remains: the clothes, the hairy skins, the food with his particular flavour. It is here that Isaac's darkened sight – that is, our senses too weak to grasp this invisible mystery of transubstantiation – finds itself deceived. Isaac indeed thinks he has Esau – or the bread – under his eyes, but all that remains are his clothes – that is, the species of bread. And under this appearance, hidden, as though disguised, is Jacob – that is, the Body of Christ. His sense of taste is also deceived, since Isaac believes he is eating Esau's food – that is, the bread – but he is only tasting its appearance. Equally deceived is the sense of smell, since Isaac thinks he smells Esau's odour – or that of the bread – which is no longer really there. Rather, he smells the odour of Esau's clothes in which Jacob is dressed – that is, the form of the bread, in which the Body of Christ is dressed.

Isaac was wise, but he is deceived by the judgement he made, believing he recognised Esau when it was really Jacob. In the same way, the exterior man in us is also deceived when judging the bread of the altar other than with faith. This is why Isaac says: "The voice is Jacob's voice, but the hands are the hands of Esau." The hands are the hands of Esau: nothing could be more false since Isaac is in fact touching the hands of Jacob. But the voice that says: "It is I" is really the voice of Jacob. Nothing could be more true. Likewise, is the Sacrament that I touch the substance of the bread? Nothing could be more false. But nothing could be more true than the voice of Jesus Christ who says, through the mouth of the priest: "This is my Body." Rebecca, that is, the soul, believes what is true, that Jacob is in the mysterious benediction – that is, that the Body of Jesus is veiled under the clothes of Esau, which is to say, under the appearance of bread.[127]

St Cyril of Jerusalem wrote: "Do not then attach yourself to the bread and wine as to natural elements, for they are, according to the declaration of the Master, Body and Blood. This is, it is true, what the senses suggest to you; but let faith reassure you."[128]

BLESSING OF JACOB		CONSECRATION	
Before the blessing	**During the blessing**	**Before the Consecration**	**During the Consecration**
Esau	Appearances of Esau (hairy skins, taste, smell)	Bread	Appearances of bread
	Jacob		Body of Christ
Isaac: *exterior man: loves Esau; deceived senses (except hearing)*		My Body: *exterior man; the deceived senses (except hearing)*	
Rebecca: *interiority: loves Jacob; undeceived heart*		My Soul: *interior man; faith that recognises the Body of Christ*	

STAGE 28

The Tree of Life Recovered

> And out of the ground the Lord God made to grow every tree that is pleasant to the sight and good for food, the tree of life also in the midst of the garden, and the tree of the knowledge of good and evil. A river flowed out of Eden to water the garden, and there it divided and became four rivers... And the Lord God commanded the man, saying, "You may freely eat of every tree of the garden; but of the tree of the knowledge of good and evil you shall not eat, for in the day that you eat of it you shall die." (*Gn* 2:9-10, 16-17)

The tree of life symbolises immortality. The tree of the knowledge of good and evil gives a privilege that God reserves for himself, namely, the faculty of deciding for himself what is good and evil and of acting accordingly. The serpent tempts Adam and Eve like this: "When you eat of it your eyes will be opened, and you will be like God, knowing good and evil" (*Gn* 3:5). This is an assertion of moral autonomy by which man denies his creaturely state and wishes to equal or be like God. It is the sin of pride, represented by the symbol of the forbidden fruit.

In the beginning, man finds himself in a perfect harmony: harmony with his Creator, harmony within himself, harmony with his neighbour, and harmony with the whole of creation:

- *With his Creator*: God seals a covenant with man (cf. *Stage 16*). He frequently visits man in the garden to speak to him.

- *Within himself*: man is created in the image of God. God saw that this was very good (*Gn* 1:31). Man's heart is whole, holy. It is neither wounded nor sullied nor divided. Man has access to the tree of life that represents immortality.

- *With his neighbour* in general, and in particular here with his wife: "Therefore a man leaves his father and his mother and clings to his wife, and they become one flesh" (*Gn* 2:24).

- *With creation*: through his work, he subdues creation by cultivating and keeping the garden (*Gn* 2:15).

This harmony is wounded by original sin:

- *With his Creator*: Adam and Eve are afraid of God. He becomes a rival: "And they heard the sound of the Lord God walking in the garden in the cool of the day, and the man and his wife hid themselves from the presence of the Lord God" (*Gn* 3:8).

• *Within himself*: the man and the woman discover that they are naked (cf. *Gn* 2:25). "The control of the soul's spiritual faculties over the body is shattered... The world is virtually inundated by sin."[129] Death makes its entrance into the history of mankind (cf. *Rm* 5:12). Through his disobedience, man cuts himself off from the tree of life: "In the day that you eat of it you shall die." God "drove out the man; and at the east of the garden of Eden he placed the cherubim, and a flaming sword which turned every way, to guard the way to the tree of life" (*Gn* 3:24).

• *With his neighbour*: interpersonal relations are subjected to tensions and divisions. The man/woman relationship is subjected to lust and domination: "Your desire shall be for your husband, and he shall rule over you" (*Gn* 3:16).

• *With creation*: creation becomes hostile, foreign. Work becomes trying and painstaking: "In toil you shall eat of it all the days of your life; thorns and thistles it shall bring forth to you" (*Gn* 3:17).

The Eucharist re-establishes what sin destroyed and reinforces the harmony desired by God at the origin:

• *With the Creator*: communion between God and men. "He who eats my flesh and drinks my blood abides in me, and I in him" (*Jn* 6:56).

• *Within himself*: although marked by the original wound, man finds peace in himself again by receiving eternal life at baptism. The Eucharist fortifies it: "He who eats my flesh and drinks my blood has eternal life" (*Jn* 6:54). The Word feeds the soul, but the Word incarnate feeds the body by giving it a seed of immortality. "With the Eucharist we digest, as it were, the 'secret' of the resurrection. For this reason St Ignatius of Antioch rightly defined the Eucharistic Bread as 'a medicine of immortality, an antidote to death.'"[130]

• *With the neighbour*: we receive the same food, we form the same body, we are animated by the same Spirit.

• *With creation*: according to Teilhard de Chardin's reflections in *The Divine Milieu*, the mystery of transubstantiation is not a change in which the Lord enters under the appearances of bread and wine. Rather it is a change in which he elevates the created realities of the bread and wine to himself, where he is found with his eternal Father. He attracts them to himself in transforming the realities of the bread and wine in an ascending spiral and converts them into his glorious Body and Blood. Thus Jesus maintains his corporeal unity by elevating to himself all these elements scattered about on earth. He leaves only the appearances of earthly realities so as not to appear glorious during the Consecration. These appearances are the vehicles of supernatural realities through which he comes physically as our food, thus attracting us to himself and letting himself be adored without manifesting his glory. This is the grace of recapitulation: All comes from God, all must return to God, all must be reconciled to Jesus, in such a way that Jesus may give back his kingdom to his Father (cf. *1 Co* 15:25).

In fact, the Eucharist is:

> [the]retribution for original sin: in the earthly paradise, the soul was deceived by the senses in tasting the forbidden fruit that appeared seductive to see and good to eat. Here, it is the senses that are deceived by what they see. Only the soul believes, and the soul alone can taste how good God is, under the trifling appearance of the bread.[131]

Also, our first parents wanted to be *gods*: "You will be like God" (*Gn* 3:5). But instead, their prideful disobedience brought them death by separating them from the tree of life and the Creator.

By contrast, the Eucharist makes us *children of God*. By the "bread of life", we become "partakers of the divine nature" (*2 P* 1:4). The dry wood of the cross, which represents sin and death, becomes the new tree of Life that bears as fruit the Eucharist, living and life-giving food. What was lost by the first sin is recovered by the Eucharist, and to a greater degree. The liturgy of Easter acclaims: "O happy fault which gained for us so great a Redeemer!" Find what more the Eucharist gives us than our first parents had before original sin.

The first pages of the Bible evoke the dramatic situation of man separated from the tree of life and, thus, subjected to the power of eternal death. The last page of the Bible, in the book of Revelation, shows how man recovers access to the tree of life: the Angel "showed me the river of the water of life, bright as crystal, flowing from the throne of God and of the Lamb through the middle of the street of the city; also, on either side of the river, the tree of life with its twelve kinds of fruit, yielding its fruit each month; and the leaves of the tree were for the healing of the nations" (*Rv* 22:1-2). "Blessed are those who wash their robes, that they may have the right to the tree of life and that they may enter the city by the gates" (*Rv* 22:14).

The river of life, bright as crystal, flows from the throne of God and of the Lamb. The Lamb evokes the sacrificial presence of Christ in the Eucharist (cf. *Stage 19*). From the throne of the Lamb, that is to say, from the Eucharist (celebrated, received, adored), flows a river of living water, healing the nations. It is the realisation of what Genesis 2:9-10 prefigured with the river divided into four branches that flowed out of the Garden of Eden and the tree of life.

This corresponds to the vision of St Faustina:

One evening upon entering my cell, I saw Jesus exposed in the monstrance. It seemed to me that this was in the open air. At the feet of Jesus, I saw my confessor and behind him a great number of dignitaries of the Church… Still farther, I saw great crowds that I could not encompass with a glance of the eye. I saw these two rays coming out from the Host, the same as in the image. They were closely united but not mixed up. They passed through the hands of my confessor, then through the hands of the clergy, from their hands to the crowd, and then returned to the Host.[132]

The Eucharist is truly a glimpse of heaven appearing on earth. It is a glorious ray of the heavenly Jerusalem which pierces the clouds of our history and lights up our journey.[133]

188

Endnotes

[1]   John Paul II, Encyclical Letter *Ecclesia de Eucharistia* (2003), no. 61.

[2]   St Peter Julian Eymard, *Adorer en Esprit et en Vérité* (Paris: Éditions F-X de Guibert, 2009), 26.

[3]   Bernadot, *De l'Eucharistie à la Trinité* (Paris: Éditions du Cerf, 1920), 15.

[4]   John Paul II, "His Heart, the Most Outstanding Sign of Love", Message of John Paul II to Archbishop Louis-Marie Billé on the One Hundredth Anniversary of the Consecration of the Human Race to the Divine Heart of Jesus (4th June 1999), in *L'Osservatore Romano*, no. 29 (21st July 1999), 6.

[5]   John Paul II, Apostolic Letter *Dominicae Cenae* (1980), no. 3.

[6]   St Thérèse of Lisieux, Letter to Marie Guérin (LT 92; 30th May 1889), *General Correspondence*, vol. 1, *1877-1890*, trans. John Clarke, O.C.D. (Washington, D.C.: ICS Publications, Institute of Carmelite Studies, 1982), 568.

[7]   St Thérèse of Lisieux, *Story of a Soul*, trans. John Clarke, O.C.D., 2nd ed. (Washington, D.C.: ICS Publications, Institute of Carmelite Studies, 1976), 14.

[8]   Ibid., 195.

[9]   St Peter Julian Eymard, *Adorer en Esprit et en Vérité* (Paris: Éditions F-X de Guibert, 2009), 22.

[10]   Paul VI, Apostolic Letter *Solemni hac Liturgia* (1968), no. 26.

[11]   Ibid.

[12]   St Margaret Mary, *Vie et Œuvres de Sainte Marguerite-Marie Alacoque*, Letter 133, to the Reverend Father Croiset (Paris: Éditions Saint-Paul, 1990), 2:487.

[13]   Ibid., Letter 97, to the Mother Superior of Saumise, end of February 1689, 2:328.

[14]   St Augustine, *Confessions*, trans. Henry Chadwick, Oxford World Classics (Oxford and New York: Oxford Univ. Press, 2009), 3.

[15]   Benedict XVI, Homily on the Solemnity of Corpus Christi, 22nd May 2008.

[16] *Catechism of the Catholic Church* (hereafter abbreviated CCC), no. 2709, quoting St Teresa of Jesus, *The Book of Her Life*, 8, 5, in *The Collected Works of St Teresa of Avila*, trans. K. Kavanaugh, O.C.D., and O. Rodriguez, O.C.D. (Washington, D.C.: ICS Publications, Institute of Carmelite Studies, 1976), 1:67.

[17] St Peter Julian Eymard, *Adorer en Esprit et en Vérité* (Paris: Éditions F-X de Guibert, 2009), 21.

[18] Father Ludovic Lécuru and Father Florian Racine, *L'adoration Eucharistique* (Paris: Éditions de l'Emmanuel, 2009), 139.

[19] Father Gaston Courtois, *Quand le Seigneur Parle au Cœur*, 13th ed. (Paris: Éditions Mediaspaul, 1993), 173.

[20] Bishop Patrick Chauvet, *Il est là! L'Adoration Eucharistique* (Saint-Maur: Éditions Parole et Silence, 2008), 92.

[21] Benedict XVI, Angelus, Corpus Christi, 10th June 2007.

[22] Anne-Françoise Vater, *Initiation à la prière et à l'adoration* (Paris: Éditions de l'Emmanuel, 2011), 152.

[23] St John Chrysostom, Homily 30, quoted in *Mois de Marie de Notre-Dame du Très Saint-Sacrement*, meditations excerpted from St Peter Julian Eymard (Paris: Librairie Ch. Poussielgue, 1982), 297.

[24] John Paul II, Apostolic Letter *Mane Nobiscum Domine* (2004), no. 18.

[25] Blessed Dina Bélanger, *Autobiographie*, ed. by the Religious of Jesus and Mary in Canada.

[26] John Paul II, Homily for the Closing of World Youth Day, Tor Vergata, Rome, 20th August 2000, nos. 4, 6.

[27] St Peter Julian Eymard, *Adorer en Esprit et en Vérité* (Paris: Éditions F-X de Guibert, 2009), 24.

[28] John Paul II, Message for the Thirty-seventh World Day of Prayer for Vocations, 14th May 2000.

[29] Benedict XVI, Homily at Marienfeld for World Youth Day in Cologne, 21st August 2005.

[30] Archbishop Fulton Sheen, quoted in the Jefferson City, Mo., *Sunday News and Tribune*, 20th December 1964, p. 7.

[31] Archbishop Fulton Sheen, "God's Quest for Man", *The Divine Romance* (1943), as quoted on CatholicCulture.org: *http://www.catholicculture.org/culture/library/view.cfm?recnum=3784*

[32] Benedict XVI, Homily at Marian Vespers with the Religious and Seminarians of Bavaria, Basilica of St Anne, Altötting, 11th September 2006.

[33] St Margaret Mary, *The Letters of St Margaret Mary Alacoque*, Letter 133, to the Reverend Father Croiset (Charlotte, N.C.: TAN Books, 1997), 234.

[34] Leo XIII, Encyclical Letter *Mirae Caritatis* (1902), no. 7.

[35] Charles de Foucauld, *Lettres à Mme de Bondy: de la Trappe à Tamanrasset* (Paris: Desclée de Brouwer, 1966), Letter of 19th January 1903.

[36] Charles de Foucauld, *Correspondances Lyonnaises (1904-1916)* (Paris: Karthala, 2005), Letter of 15th December 1904.

[37] Charles de Foucauld, *Lettres à Mme de Bondy*, Letter of 19th January 1903.

[38] Ibid., Letter of 18th November 1907.

[39] Ibid., Letter of 16th December 1905.

[40] Charles de Foucauld, Diary, 8th July 1903.

[41] St Damien of Molokai, *Un Étrange Bonheur* (Paris: Éditions du Cerf, 1994), Letter to his brother, 13th December 1881.

[42] Sister Josefa Menendez, *The Way of Divine Love, or the Message of the Sacred Heart to the World, and a Short Biography of His Messenger* (Charlotte, N.C.: Saint Benedict Press, 2006), 271-72.

[43] St Peter Julian Eymard, *Adorer en Esprit et en Vérité* (Paris: Éditions F-X de Guibert, 2009), 178.

[44] Ibid., 182.

[45] St Anthony Mary Claret, *Un Quart d'Heure en Présence du Saint Sacrement* (Hauteville: Éditions du Parvis, 1988).

[46] St John Chrysostom, *Homily on Saint Matthew*, 82, 4.

[47] John Paul II, Letter to Bishop Albert Houssiau of Liège for the 750th anniversary of Corpus Christi, 28th May 1996.

[48] Paul VI, Discourse for the Inauguration of International Eucharistic Social Works at Dos Hermanas.

[49] John Paul II, Letter on the Mystery and Worship of the Eucharist *Dominicae Cenae*, 24th February 1980, no. 3.

[50] The expression "soixante-huitard" (literally, "sixty-eighter") is a noun and adjective referring to the socio-political upheavals marked by a radical revolutionary spirit that began in France in May 1968 and spread throughout much of Western Europe. – trans.

[51] Pascal Pingault, *Fioretti du Pain de Vie* (Paris: Éditions Le Sarment-Fayard, 1986), 79-80.

[52] Peter Kreeft, *The Angels and the Ants: Bringing Heaven Closer to Your Daily Life* (Ann Arbor, Mich.: Servant Publications, 1994), 92.

[53] St Anthony Mary Claret, *Un Quart d'Heure en Présence du Saint Sacrement* (Hauteville: Éditions du Parvis, 1988).

[54] Benedict XVI, Encyclical Letter *Deus Caritas Est* (2006), English translation: *God Is Love* (San Francisco: Ignatius Press, 2006), no. 36, pp. 89-90.

[55] St Mother Teresa, *Tu m'Apportes l'Amour*, Écrits *Spirituels* (Paris: Éditions du Centurion, 1975).

[56] Ibid.

[57] Ibid.

[58] Ibid.

[59] Ibid.

[60] Ibid.

[61] St Peter Julian Eymard, *Adorer en Esprit et en Vérité* (Paris: Éditions F-X de Guibert, 2009), 101-2.

[62] Benedict XVI, Post-synodal Apostolic Exhortation *Sacramentum Caritatis* (2007), no. 66.

[63] Benedict XVI, Angelus, Castel Gandolfo: 28th August 2005, recalling his Address at the Meeting with German Bishops in the Piussaal of the Seminary in Cologne during World Youth Day (21st August 2005).

[64] Benedict XVI, *Sacramentum Caritatis*, no. 66.

[65] Benedict XVI, Homily for Corpus Christi, Rome: 22nd May 2008.

[66] Paul VI, Encyclical Letter *Mysterium Fidei* on the Holy Eucharist (1965), nos. 38-39.

[67] Leo XIII, Encyclical Letter *Mirae Caritatis* (1902), no. 7.

[68] Cardinal Journet, *Entretiens sur l'Eucharistie* (Saint-Maur: Parole et Silence, 2000), 51-56.

[69] The firmament represents the apparent "vault" of the sky, which was for the ancient Semites, a solid dome, holding back the waters above. Through its openings the flood will stream down (cf. *Gn* 7:11).

[70] CCC 1.

[71] John Paul II, Message for the 37th World Day of Prayer for Vocations, 14th May 2000.

[72] St Augustine, sermon 227, 1; PL 38:1099.

[73] St Augustine, PL 35:1568.

[74] St Augustine, PL 35:1622.

[75] John Paul II, General Audience, "Eucharist Is Perfect Sacrifice of Praise", 11th October 2000.

[76] A traditional Catholic prayer dating back at least to the fourteenth century (perhaps Pope John XXII) and often attributed incorrectly to St Ignatius of Loyola. – trans.

[77] Benedict XVI, Homily, World Youth Day, Cologne, Marienfeld, 21st August 2005.

[78] Cardinal Journet, *Le Mystère de l'Eucharistie* (Paris: Pierre Téqui, 1981), 32-33.

[79] John Paul II, Encyclical Letter *Ecclesia de Eucharistia* (2003), no. 12.

[80] Théodelinde Dubouché, *L'Adoration au Soleil de Dieu: Fragments Spirituels*, ed. Sisters of the Adoration of Reparation, p. 40.

[81] St Peter Julian Eymard, *Adorer en Esprit et Vérité* (Paris: F-X de Guibert, 2009), 37.

[82] Ibid., 101-2.

83 Ibid., 261.

84 Ibid., 257.

85 Ibid., 53.

86 John Paul II, Apostolic Letter *Dominicae Cenae* (1980), no. 7.

87 St Faustina, *Petit Journal*, 300.

88 Ibid., 1484.

89 St Peter Julian Eymard, *Adorer en Esprit et Vérité*, 102.

90 John Paul II, Encyclical Letter *Redemptor Hominis* (1979), no. 20.

91 St Ambrose, *Sur Saint Luc*, II, 87; PL 15:1585, (Paris: Éditions du Cerf, 1958).

92 Brother Emmanuel Perrier, O.P., for Liberté-Politique.com; cf. CCC 1601ff.; Vatican Council II, *Gaudium et Spes* (1965), nos. 47ff.; Apostolic Exhortation *Familiaris Consortio* (1981), nos. 11ff., 20 on indissolubility.

93 Vatican Council II, Decree *Presbyterorum Ordinis* (1965), no. 5.

94 John Paul II, Encyclical Letter *Ecclesia de Eucharistia* (2003), no. 5.

95 Joseph Ratzinger, Declaration *Dominus Iesus* (2000), no. 16.

96 Ibid., no. 20; quotation from Vatican Council II, Dogmatic Constitution *Lumen Gentium* (1964), no. 14.

97 Ibid.; quotation from John Paul II, Encyclical Letter *Redemptoris Missio* (1990), no. 10.

98 Ibid., no. 21; quotation from Vatican Council II, Decree *Ad Gentes* (1975), no. 7.

99 John Paul II, *Ecclesia de Eucharistia*, no. 6.

100 St Peter Julian Eymard, *La Divine Eucharistie*, 2nd series, 15th ed. (Paris: Desclée de Brouwer, 1922), 146.

101 John Paul II, *Ecclesia de Eucharistia*, no. 22.

102 Ibid., no. 16.

103 CCC 1650.

104 John Paul II, Apostolic Exhortation *Familiaris Consortio* (1981), no. 84.

105 Ibid.

[106] Ibid.

[107] John Paul II, Letter to Bishop Houssiau for the 750th anniversary of Corpus Christi, 28th May 1996.

[108] CCC 169, quoting Faustus of Riez, *De Spiritu Sancto* 1, 2: PL 62:11.

[109] Catherine de Bar (Mechtilde of the Blessed Sacrament), *Adorer et Adhérer* (Paris: Cerf, 1994), 102.

[110] Homily on the First Letter to the Corinthians 24, 2: PG 61:200, quoted in John Paul II, *Ecclesia de Eucharistia*, no. 23.

[111] John Paul II, *Ecclesia de Eucharistia*, no. 24.

[112] St Peter Julian Eymard, *Adorer en Esprit et Vérité* (Paris: Éditions F-X de Guibert, 2009), 99.

[113] St Thérèse of Lisieux, *Story of a Soul: The Autobiography of St Thérèse of Lisieux*, trans. John Clark, O.C.D., 2nd ed. (Washington, D.C.: ICS Publications, Institute of Carmelite Studies, 1976), 14, 195.

[114] Conference by Bishop Léonard during the Congress of Adoration, Paray-le-Monial, 2005.

[115] St Peter Julian Eymard, *Adorer en Esprit et en Vérité*, 53.

[116] John Paul II, Letter to Bishop Houssiau for the 750th anniversary of Corpus Christi, 28th May 1996.

[117] Father Anthony Birot, the House of Trinitarian Love community, conference on *L'Eucharistie comme Mystère Trinitaire* at the colloquium *Communion-Évangélisation* (Hyères: 19th April 2009). The author has since developed this whole point, with its theological references, in *La Dramatique Trinitaire de l'Amour* (Saint-Maur: Parole et Silence-Lethielleux, 2009), 100-113.

[118] Vatican Council II, Dogmatic Constitution *Dei Verbum* (1964), no. 5; the quote is in fact from the Second Council of Orange, canon 7.

[119] Ibid., no. 2.

[120] St Augustine, *Confessions* VII, 10, 16.

[121] CCC 166.

[122] Ibid., 157, quoting, first: St Thomas Aquinas, *Summa Theologiae* II-